The Mystery Fancier

Volume 5 Number 1
January/February 1981

The MYSTERY FANcier

Volume 5 Number 1
January/February, 1981

TABLE OF CONTENTS

MYSTERIOUSLY SPEAKING 1
Spy Series Characters in Hardback, Part VI,
    by Barry Van Tilburg. 2
Hunter and Hunted, by Jane S. Bakerman. 3
The Body in the Library, by Martin Morse Wooster. 11
Blame Stephen Sondheim, by E.F. Bleiler 15
IT'S ABOUT CRIME, by Marvin Lachman 17
MYSTERY*FILE: Short Reviews by Steve Lewis. 20
THE DOCUMENTS IN THE CASE (Letters) 30

The MYSTERY FANcier
(USPS:428-590)
is edited and published bi-monthly by Guy M. Townsend,
29 S. Church Street, West Chester, Pennsylvania 19380.
Contributions of all descriptions are welcomed.

SUBSCRIPTION RATES: Domestic second class mail, $12.00 per year (6 issues); overseas surface mail, $12.00; overseas airmail, $15.00. Overseas subscribers please pay in international money order, check drawn on U.S. bank, or currency; no checks drawn of foreign banks, please.

Second class postage paid at West Chester, Pennsylvania.

Copyright 1981 by Guy M. Townsend
All rights reserved for contributors
ISSN:0146-3160

Mysteriously Speaking...

You might call this the R. Jeff Banks Memorial Issue of TMF--not, I hasten to clarify, that Jeff has departed this world for a better one (or, quite possibly, a worse one). Rather, because it is filled virtually to overflowing with his favorite feature--letters.

We have gone from dearth to deluge in only two issues, and I for one am delighted. It is highly unlikely--and, probably, equally undesirable--that this superfluity of letters will continue as a regular thing, but it's good to know that interest hasn't waned among the faithful.

There were so many letters this time around that a couple of things got squeezed out. You index fans will be delighted to hear that David Doerrer has sent me his annual index to books reviewed in the just-past volume of TMF, together with a supplement of all the books reviewed or mentioned in Marvin's columns since volume two. Steve Lewis is back, as I am sure everyone is pleased to note, but the other reviews got bumped, including a review of the Rex Stout bibliography, to my great regret.

With some luck (not a great deal, really) this issue could be in the mail by the end of February, which will put TMF back on schedule (if you accept the rather loose interpretation that a bi-monthly magazine is on schedule so long as it is mailed within either of the two months on the cover). With some cooperation from you folks, in shooting those letters, reviews, and articles off to me as soon as you receive this issue, it's just barely possible (no promises, of course) that I'll be able to get the March/April issue out by the end of March. Who knows?--the time may eventually come when TMF once again comes out at the beginning of it's two-month period.

For a number of issues now, I have been waffling on the issue of putting punctuation inside or outside of quotation marks. I still contend, and will forever do so, that logic dictates the inclusion of punctuation within quotation marks only when the punctuation is part of the quoted matter, but I've finally concluded that there's nothing to be gained from swimming against this particular stream; being unable to beat them, I've decided to goin them. What the hell, there'll be other windmills ....

My latest move has occasioned the by now accustomed amount of comment, with a few horse jokes being thrown in to provide a little novelty. I have now [*continued at bottom of page 2*]

SPY SERIES CHARACTERS IN HARDBACK, VI
By Barry Van Tilburg

DOSSIER #37: Denis Nayland Smith.
CREATED BY: Sax Rohmer (Arthur Sarsfield Ward).
OCCUPATION: Starts the series as a Chief Superintendent and when war breaks out works for British Intelligence.
ASSOCIATES: Dr. Petrie, Smith's Dr. Watson; Kerrigan, Smith's helper in later books; Dr. Fu Manchu, Smith's genius Chinese archenemy whom he admires.
WEAPONS: Smith carries a service revolver, usually a Webley.
OTHER COMMENTS: Smith is very like Sherlock Holmes. He has a doctor who writes his adventurous memoirs. He is a nervous individual who paces a lot and gets lost in his thoughts. He fights an arch criminal who has a vast organization (the Si-Fan). The books often have a science-fiction quality about them. In *The Drums of Fu Manchu*, Smith has to deal with Zombies. Nigel Green and Peter Sellers have portrayed Smith in movies.

The Insidious Dr. Fu Manchu (McBride, 1913; published as *The Mystery of Dr. Fu Manchu* by Collier, 1913).
The Return of Dr. Fu Manchu (McBride, 1916; published as *The Devil Doctor* by Collier, 1916).
The Hand of Fu Manchu (McBride, 1917; published as *The Si-Fan Mysteries* by Collier, 1917).
The Daughter of Fu Manchu (Collier, 1930; McBride, 1931).
The Mask of Fu Manchu (Doubleday, 1932).
Fu Manchu's Bride (Doubleday, 1933; published as *The Bride of Fu Manchu* by Cassell, 1933).
The Trail of Fu Manchu (Doubleday, 1934).
President Fu Manchu (Doubleday, 1936).
The Drums of Fu Manchu (Doubleday, 1940).
The Fu Manchu Book (Cassell, 1940).
The Island of Fu Manchu (Cassell, 1941).
Shadow of Fu Manchu (Collier, 1948; Doubleday, 1948).
Re-Enter Dr. Fu Manchu (Jenkins, 1957).
Emperor Fu Manchu (Jenkins, 1959).
The Wrath of Fu Manchu (Stacey, 1973).

[*continued from page 1*] gotten settled into a third-floor apartment above a florist's shop in downtown West Chester, a scant two blocks from where the practical horses are stabled, so everyone note the slight change in address from care of *Practical Horseman*, 225 S. Church St., to just plain 29 S. Church St. It is to that new address, fellow fanciers, that your articles, reviews, letters, and charitable donations should now be sent. I'll still get mail addressed to 225 S. Church, but--since I always drop everything to read whatever you folks send me--I'll get more work done at the office if you send your mail to my home address. This latest move came a couple of months too late for me to make it to the Nero Wolfe gathering (and the party at Otto's for the Stout bibliography), but you folks along the eastern seaboard are hereby warned that, now that I am within convenient striking distance, you are likely to see my squint-eyed visage (not to mention my short, tubby form and flowing red beard) at mystery-related gatherings, so watch it.

HUNTER AND HUNTED

Comparison and Contrast in Tony Hillerman's
People of Darkness

By Jane S. Bakerman

Avid fans of Tony Hillerman's Lieutenant Joe Leaphorn series will find plenty of familiar territory and material in Hillerman's latest novel, *People of Darkness* (New York: Harper & Row, 1980), despite the introduction of a new protagonist, Sergeant Jim Chee. Both Leaphorn and Chee are members of the Navajo Tribal Police, though the younger Chee works out of Crownpoint Station. There is even one reference to Captain Leaphorn at Chinle, indicating a promotion for Joe, though the reader's attention is turned away from him for this novel.

Hillerman is fairly detailed about Chee's background. Members of his family are much more openly discussed than are the shadowy Leaphorns, but the author has saved plenty of information for later revelation and character development, just in case the Chee books also become a series (and readers will hope they do). Most prominent among Chee's relatives seems to be his uncle, Hosteen Frank Sam Nakai, one of the many prominent singers the family has produced, more "than any of the other more than sixty Navajo clans" (p. 61). Nakai, performer of the Night Chant, the Enemy Way, and "key parts of several other curing ceremonials," also teaches ceremonialism at Navajo Community College at Rough Rock (p. 61). We know also that it was he who gave Chee his "war name," Long Thinker. All this about a character who never appears in the action but who figures very prominently in Chee's thoughts amounts to more solid facts than are revealed about Leaphorn, protagonist in three novels of his own (*The Blessing Way*, 1970; *Dance Hall of the Dead*, 1973; and *Listening Woman*, 1978).

But in other respects, the biographies of the two men are similar. Like Leaphorn a member of the Slow Talking Dinee clan, Chee is also a man trapped between two worlds. His early training is, of course, Navajo, and he, too, has gone away to boarding school and later earned a degree in anthropology. At the university, he's learned to be suspicious of white women:

> Chee recognized the look. He had seen it often at the University of New Mexico--and most often among Anglo coeds enrolled in Native American Studies courses. The courses attracted Anglo students, largely female, enjoying racial/ethnic guilt trips. Chee had concluded early that their interest was more in Indian males than in Indian mythology. Their eyes asked if you were really any different from the blond boys they had grown up with. (p. 66)

The wariness is, however, only one part of a larger problem. As a member of a minority group constantly influenced and often threatened by the white culture, Chee has been taught to study the majority in order to understand its pattern--if he can.

> But Jim Chee didn't understand the thinking of the whites. Neither Changing Woman nor Talking God had given him a song to produce that understanding. What would his uncle say to that? Chee knew exactly what the old man would say. He could almost hear him, because he had heard him so often:
> "Boy, when you understand the big, you understand the little. First understand the big."
> And that would mean, in this case, that if Chee learned to understand all men (the big), he could understand white men (the little). His uncle would add that if a Navajo could find harmony with a deer, he could find equal harmony with a white man.... And then his uncle, who never failed to belabor a point, would add some wisdom about deer and men. He would say that the deer is much like the Navajo in fundamental ways. It loves its offspring and its mate, food, water, and its rest. And it hates cold, hunger, pain, and death. But the deer is also different. Its life is short. It builds no hogans. The Navajo is more like a white man than a deer.
> That's what his uncle would say, Chee thought sourly. But his uncle had no dealings with the whites when he could avoid them. (p. 170)

Chee cannot avoid the whites; they influence his work as well as his world, and like Leaphorn he continues to strive to understand them in order to be an efficient policeman and a man who protects his integrity.

With that effort toward understanding, of course, comes, as it does to Leaphorn, a constant sense of the racism in American life. Chee finds some in himself--he's trying to overcome the habit of "seeing all non-Navajos as looking very much alike" (p. 118)--and he certainly finds it among white law enforcement officers. One example occurs when an Indian reports that his father's corpse has disappeared from a major cancer center:

> He imagined Charley showing up at the Albuquerque police building, trying to find somebody to take the report, telling a clerk (would the clerk have been incredulous or merely bored?) of a missing body taken by a witch. What would the crime have been? At worst, transporting a cadaver with a permit from the medical examiner. And the police would have guessed it was merely a mix-up: the body claimed by another relative, a family feud, perhaps. And Thomas Charley wouldn't have raised hell and pressed for answers. He already knew two answers. One was that nobody would pay much attention to a Navajo trying to raise hell. And the other was that a witch had flown away with the body. Still, Chee felt his anger rising at this indignity. (p. 71)

Both Navajo officers are self-controlled men, however, and Chee no more lets his anger dominate him than Leaphorn does.

The two men are alike in one other important way that enhances the novels; they are responsive to the stunning natural beauty which surrounds them. Hillerman uses this trait in several ways. Obviously, it deepens the characterizations of his protagonists, and further, it lends an element of lyricism to the otherwise very realistic plots. It also, as in this passage, helps to symbolize the difficulty of Chee's efforts to straddle two cultures:

> The sun had dropped behind the horizon, but the top of the moun-

> tain, rising a mile above the valley floor, still caught the direct light. Tsoodzil, the Navajos called it, the Turquoise Mountain. It was one of the four sacred peaks which First Man had built to guard Dinetah. He had built it on a blue blanket of earth carried up from the underworld, and decorated it with turquoise and blue flint. And then he had pinned it to the earth with a magic knife, and assigned Turquoise Girl to live there and Big Snake to guard her until the Fourth World ended. Now it appeared the magic knife had slipped. The sacred mountain seemed to float in the sky, cut off from the solid earth by the ground haze. (p. 29)

Clearly, Hillerman also exploits Chee's quick response to beauty and nature to insert some of the Indian lore which so enriches his tales. The material is never falsely introduced; it is always very, very well integrated, and it unfailingly serves to emphasize Chee's background and to highlight the duality of his situation:

> Except for the east, the clouds were gone and the night sky, swept clean of dust, was ablaze with starlight. Chee stood for a moment, enjoying it. He hunted out the autumn constellations--the formations that rose from the south as the earth tilted to end summer and begin the Season When the Thunder Sleeps. Chee knew them not by the names the Greeks and Romans had given them, but from his grandfather. Now he picked out the Spider Woman (named Acquarius by the Romans), low on the southern horizon, and the mischievous Blue Flint Boys, whom the Greeks called the Pleiades, just above the blackness of the storm against the northeast sky. Almost directly overhead was Born of Water, the philosophical member of the Hero Twins. Over his right shoulder, surrounded by stars of lesser magnitude, soared the Blue Heron. According to the Origin Myth as told in Chee's clan, it had been Heron whom First Man had sent back into the flooding underworld to rescue the forgotten witchcraft bundle and thus bring evil into the surface world. (pp. 17-18)

Finally, Chee, like Leaphorn, devotes his life to working against law-breakers. He remarks, "We don't have much violence, we Navajos. What there is is mostly associated with witchcraft. Changing Woman taught us how to cope with the Navajo Wolves. We turn the evil around so that it works against the witch" (p. 188). This comment, the idea that evil is properly handled when it is turned against the witch, is the theme of *People of Darkness,* just as it is the theme of the Leaphorn novels. The Navajo way is to seek harmony, to find the pattern, and Chee, like Joe Leaphorn, sets about restoring the pattern after it has been shattered by an evildoer. He turns the evil against the witch.

Chee's introductory case begins when wealthy Rosemary Vines hires him to recover a box of her sick husband's "keepsakes," items she claims were stolen. She maintains that the People of Darkness, a branch of the peyote church, have stolen the box. Intuitively wary of Rosemary Vines' attitude, Chee is even more perplexed--and intrigued--when Gordo Sena, the Valencia County Sheriff, and B.J. Vines, himself, warn him off the case. Eventually, a pretty Anglo, Mary Landon, the peyote church, and one of Hillerman's deadliest villains, hired killer Colton Wolf, also become involved, and the chase is on, leading Chee through three puzzles. What is in the missing box? Why are members of the Charley family (headmen of the peyote cult) so prone to early deaths from cancer? And what has the current investigation to do with an oil-drilling accident which took place a generation earlier? Hillerman handles all these plot complications very skillfully and enhances this extended chase with one final element which is its most fascinating motif.

Throughout the story, Chee, in seeking a solution to the mystery, tracks the hired killer. Meanwhile, to protect his identity and his livelihood, Colton Wolf stalks Chee and Mary Landon. Both men are hunters; both are hunted. The hunt is thrilling, and it is symbolized in a memory from Wolfe's youth which identifies the pattern by which he lives and the pattern by which *People of Darkness* is organized: "He'd had two marbles then and the marbles would chase one another down the cracks [in the linoleum-covered floor]. He could remember playing that game endlessly, day after day" (p. 165). Wolfe still plays that game, now a deadly one, and Chee is forced to play it with him.

Just as Chee can be compared with Leaphorn,* he can also be compared--and contrasted--with Wolf. This pattern lends the novel the final Hillerman touch, for here, as in all four of his earlier mysteries, Hillerman offers not only a good puzzle, not only a whacking good chase, but also a serious and effective study in human nature. Chee and Wolf stand, of course, for Good and Evil, for Order and Disorder, but they are not simply stereotypical tools of the plot. Each is a fully realized character, and each is facing a turning point in his career. This career crisis is their most important similarity.

Both men are very good at their jobs; both display a certain intensity in setting about their work, and both perceive their careers as ways of life as well as means of earning their keep, but both are thinking of change. Jim Chee is considering moving into a career with the FBI; his change would be voluntary. Clayton Wolf is threatened with a change from the outside; he's botched one assassination, and Jim Chee has seen him; his career and his independence may be ruined.

Chee has only four more weeks in which to make his decision, and it's enormously difficult. To take the new job is to leave the area he loves, but it also means abandoning his Navajo heritage: "As a matter of fact, you couldn't be both a Navajo and an FBI agent. You couldn't be a Navajo away from the People" (p. 78). The decision is complicated by still another factor. Not only is Chee deeply rooted in his people's Way, he's also potentially important in the preservation of their traditions. For much of his life, he's wanted to become a *yataalii*--"the anthropologists called them shamans, and most people around the reservation called them singers, or medicine men," though "none of these expressions really fit the role" (p. 6). By any name, the role is crucial to the ongoing life

---

*Certainly, *People of Darkness* can stand alone; it is enjoyable in its own right, and readers need not have read the Leaphorn books as background. At the same time, Hillerman seems to have made a conscious effort to show the similarities between the protagonists. In doing so, he has, as it were, underscored the accuracy of the Navajo habits of thought, living, and belief depicted in the earlier novels.

of his people and, Chee suspects, central to his personal identity; his talent is extremely strong, and becoming a singer will mean carrying on the tradition of his mother's family and of his clan.

Chee has begun studying to be a singer, and he recognizes that what he has learned helps him in his work, in this hunt, and in achieving individuality:

> His confidence surprised him. But he *was* confident. [The quest] involved things purely Navajo--a pattern of thinking and behavior with which Chee was in intimate harmony.... For all enterprises, such harmony was essential. Especially for the hunter. And this was from the very start a hunt.
> One of the prayers from the Stalking Way ran through his mind, and the voice of his uncle chanting it:
>> *I am the Black God as I sing this,*
>> *Black God I am. I come and I stand*
>> *beneath the East, beneath the Turquoise*
>> *Mountain.*
>> *The crystal doe walks toward me,*
>> *as I call it, as I pray to it,*
>> *toward me it comes walking, understanding*
>> *me*
>> *it walks this day into my right hand.* (p. 169)

Much later, as the complex hunt nears its climax, Chee realizes that his uncle's teachings and the chants themselves offer him the courage as well as the skill that arises from understanding the pattern.

> Chee felt an impatience to move, to begin the contest. It was much darker, but not quite dark enough. Words from the Stalking Way ran through his memory, his uncle's husky voice singing them, his uncle's stubby fingers tapping rhythm on the pot drum.
>> *I am the Black God, arising with the twilight,*
>> *a part of the twilight.*
>> *Out from the West, out from the Darkness*
>> *Mountain, a buck of dark flint stands*
>> *out before me.*
>> *The best male game of darkness, it calls to me,*
>> *it hears my voice calling.*
>> *Our calls become one in beauty.*
>> *As I, the Black God, go toward it.*
>> *As the male game of darkness comes toward*
>> *me.*
>> *With beauty before us, we come together.*
>> *That my arrow may free its sacred breath.*
>> *That my arrow may bring its death in*
>> *beauty.*
> The song ran on and on in Chee's mind, a pattern of repetitions, of slightly varied sounds and slightly varied meanings, exorcising the primal dread of death and preparing man and animal for the sacred hunt.
> Jimmy Chee was ready. (pp. 180-181)

As the action progresses, and as the plot nears its climax, readers come to understand Jimmy Chee better and better. Basic to that understanding is a growing awareness of Chee's firm grounding in the Navajo Way. As the young man chooses between staying with the People or joining the majority culture, readers grow anxious. One of the qualities that makes Chee such a good tracker, such a good policeman, is his harmony with his background. It makes him responsive to the Indians he deals with in his work, and in this story it both arms him and sharpens his understanding of the whites whose incursions into Indian culture trigger the crimes. If Chee is correct, if he can't be a Navajo *and* an FBI man, what will happen to his professional skills? Should they be blunted, would the "new" Chee, a man who would have abandoned his heritage, have any identity at all?

Though Wolf, like Chee, is coping with a career crisis, he is not helped by any sense of background or roots. In fact, his very lack of a heritage appears to be the factor that is damaging the killer's intense concentration and shadowing his heretofore brilliant, if murderous, career. Colton Wolf has, in fact, no identity at all. An abused, abandoned child, he has only a few memories of his youth:

> Colton was aware that things were wrong with his memory. Gaps in it. He ran his thumb down his sweater, feeling the bump under the skin where the rib had healed crookedly. He could remember when he didn't have the bump--when they lived in San Diego. He could remember having it, already healed, in Bakersfield. But he couldn't remember the beating that produced it. It was the same with the ridge of thick white scar tissue under the hair above his left ear. That also had grown from some blank spot in his childhood. The last time he had tried to remember about that was in Taylorville, but trying had made him sick.... (pp. 165-166)

What memories Wolf does have of his childhood are grim, the principal one being of the day he was abandoned. At one point, he thinks about one of the few childhood homes he can recall among the many in which he and his mother lived:

> The last time he had seen it was the day after his twelfth birthday--the last time he had come home. The boy he knew at school had said he couldn't stay at his house any longer and he had walked hime to see if Buddy Shaw [his mother's lover] had sobered up, and if Buddy Shaw would let him return. He had found the house empty. He had peered through the windows and seen the kitchen stripped of his mother's pans, and the bathroom stripped of her toiletries. But in the room where he slept, his things were still scattered. The bed-clothing was gone from the cot, but the blue jacket his mother had got for him somewhere was still hanging on its peg. And his books were there. And his cap. He had broken a window and gone inside, cutting his hand in his panic. There had been nothing except the old furniture that had been there when they moved in and his own spare clothing. (pp. 48-49)

Wolf is presently engaged in an intense search for his mother, racking his memory and employing a private detective, an operative he never sees but communicates with only by mail, and in his view, even that distanced communication is dangerous. Normally, he interacts with almost no one except "Boxholder," the telephone voice through which he gets his assignments:

> It wasn't that Colton Wolf expected any mail. It was part of

> the routine by which he lived. In whatever town he parked his
> trailer, Colton immediately rented a post office box. He rented
> it in the name of whatever commercial-sounding noun that came to
> mind. Then he mailed a note to Boxholder at a post office box
> number in El Paso, Texas, in which he reported his new address.
> That was Colton's link to the man who provided him with his assign-
> ments. It was his only link with the world. (p. 44)

The assignments are killings-for-hire, and his occupation as well as his rootlessness make Wolf one of the most isolated characters in fiction. Like Jimmy Chee, he straddles two worlds, the world which exists inside and the world which exists outside the law, but unlike Chee, Wolf belongs to neither. Chee is the product of a sizeable family, of a huge clan, and of an indentifiable people. Wolf has no one, and his identity is empty. Not only has he no known parent, but also he has no true name; he's simply chosen

> a neutral name for himself. He'd use it only until he could find
> his mother. She'd tell him his real name. She'd tell him about
> his father, and his grandparents. And about the family home. It
> would be a small town, Colton thought, and there'd be a graveyard
> with tombstones for the family. When he found her, she'd tell
> him who he was. Until then, he'd pick a last name. Something
> simple. He picked Wolf. (p. 48)

What Wolf seeks is his place in the ordinary white world, a world from which he'd been banished when his mother allowed her lover to drive the boy from their shabby home. Her subsequent disappearance is the ultimate symbol of Wolf's rootlessness, and it's almost impossible to picture this deadly, silent killer settling back into the American Dream of the small town, the quiet, sane, "normal" background. It's much easier to understand Wolf's dedication to his profession--he's amoral (who would have taught him a code of ethics?), he's passionless (except for his desperate need to find his mother), and he's mechanical (living according to a rigid schedule in both his professional and personal lives).

Chee, on the other hand, is a man of disciplined impulse. True, he precipitously moves ahead in this case though he's been thoroughly warned and threatened off, but he does so within the discipline of the laws of both tribe and dominant culture. Also impulsively, he courts Mary Landon, a white woman, even though he knows very well the complexity such a relationship must engender. Yet, he approaches the courtship with caution, testing Mary's ability to understand his way of life--and never (at least as yet) tells her his secret war name becuase he's not yet ready to share his most intimate identity.

With no identity to risk, Colton Wolfe is free to be an outlaw; with every identity to lose, Jim Chee tries to measure the freedom he may or may not have to align himself totally with white law, the FBI. And through these balances, through these motifs, Hillerman weaves the comparisons and contrasts between protagonist and antagonist against the extended pattern of Jim Chee's likenesses to Joe Leaphorn.

The complex but independent pattern of this story offers a very satisfying "read." The extended pattern also satisfies the expectations of fans Tony Hillerman has won through his Joe Leaphorn novels. Both patterns ask important questions about contemporary American life, suggest thoughtful answers without sacrificing a jot of action or suspense. Taken all in all, then, *People of Darkness* is a fine contribution to the Tony Hillerman canon, confirming its author's reputation as an excellent writer.

THE BODY IN THE LIBRARY
TWENTIETH-CENTURY CRIME AND MYSTERY WRITERS AND THE MYSTERY WORLD IN OUR TIME

By Martin Morse Wooster

How do you review a monument?
It's easy to throw superlatives at this book; the praise it has gotten, and will get, from the amateur and professional mystery journals is well-deserved. But to throw another bouquet at this volume is as useful as reiterating the nitpicking criticism that, because such-and-such an author has been excluded, the book suffers mightily; if anything, the book pushes in the direction of inclusiveness rather than exclusiveness. There are problems with the organizational scheme, the chief of which is a rather odd rule. As I understand it, an author is listed under the pseudonym that he or she first used. Thus the British writer Henry Patterson is listed under "Marlowe, Hugh," rather than under "Higgins, Jack" or "Patterson, Harry", pseudonyms of both far more use and recognition than the obscure Marlowe name. But these are, at best, minor criticisms, at worst, irrelevant ones. For the problem with a book of this sort, packed with enormous amounts of information, is that it transcends the limits of a reviewer's knowledge, so that the critic is reduced to a sort of idel boastfullness, a literary one-upmanship that reduces the critic as it baffles the reader. This is why Allen Hubin's *Bibliography of Crime Fiction* has never received the critical attention that it deserves; no critic, to my knowledge, has the enthusiasm and skill to challenge Hubin at his own game.

Thus what follows is not, as such, a review of *Twentieth-Century Crime and Mystery Writers*. I will, instead, discuss how this book freezes mystery criticism and the mystery world in as effective a cross-section as a shellacked piece of sequoia preserves the growth of a tree.

In the world of mystery fiction, there are three groups that can be plucked from the morass: the fans, the pros, and the academics. These subdivisions are not, of course, exact, and the kaleidoscope of permutations and combinations that ensue could create a paper of its own. Even that quintessentially fannish organization DAPA-EM has contributors in this volume as diverse as Kathi Maio and Art Scott.

The distinguishing feature of the three groups is the way that a member of each would view the texts under discussion. Here are three representative sentences:

> If the novels communicate an overall impression of restraint, it is, perhaps, that of their period--or, at any rate, of what we modern readers imagine the period to be.

> His creation was Hildegarde Withers, a snoopy old maid sleuth extraordinaire.

> [Blank] is a popular writer in the best sense of the term, a precise craftsman who always manages to reveal depth behind the smooth commercial surface of his work.

These are three ways of viewing a given writer's output. The first sentence sees a novel as part of a given *oeuvre* in much the same way as a canned ham comes out of a pig: untraceable to any given pig, but clean and presumably tasty nonetheless. The second focuses on the creation of a given author: the writer as myth-builder. The third sees the subject as a fellow professional, and rallies behind him in an act of patriotic defense, a closing of the ranks. Text, character, pro: academic, fan, writer. I have, admittedly, made these differences to be broader than they actually are; but the distinctions are, I trust, workable ones from which we can proceed.

The writing from fans is, at its best, solid appreciation, at its worst, dull praise. The sturdiness of a Briney, the diligence of a Nevins, the steadfast ferreting around of a Shibuk are much to be desired. At its worst, fannish writing tends towards clichés, as in one essay where we learn that one writer's "talent for the bizarre stems from his bizarre life," no doubt producing a career "as an outstanding stylist capable of producing startling images." At least that detective did not suffer the fate of another poor soul, doomed to "roam the hilly streets of San Francisco," no doubt trying to find a nice flat place to park.

As for the professionals, their output tends to be more along the police-procedural rather than the amateur-detective school of criticism--facts unilluminated by insight. That many of the writers under discussion probably do not need extensive analysis--*viz*., most of Bill Pronzini's articles on relatively obscure (save to the collectors) hard-boiled writers--does not exempt from this generalization H.R.F. Keating, whose splendid essays on a wide variety of Britons are the most interesting and most important criticism in this book.

But the most wrong-headed (and, for that reason, most illuminating) of the criticism in this book comes from the academics. "Academic" is, of course, a catch-all phrase, and because a writer possesses tenure at a university does not mean that he or she is eternally doomed to produce pedantic prose. But, as fans tend towards idolatry, so do academics tend towards elevation of the readable to the dull.

It is, of course, hard to pick out the single worst essay in this volume. There are so many bad essays that one finds it rather hard to pick a particular writer that descends into the depths with more regularity than any other. I have, however, found a writer who combines the two worst characteristics of the academic--prolixity and fatuousness--to a degree that her competitors cannot match. Her name is Joanne Harack Hayne; she is described as "Co-Ordinator, Programme Development, School of Continuing Studies, University of Toronto"-- i.e., she determines the fate of returning dropouts. She has chosen to enlighten us on such writers as Mary Roberts Rinehart and Christianna Brand; but let us examine her essay on Peter Lovesey, an essay I regard as the worst piece of criticism in the book.

You may have thought Lovesey to be an engaging social historian, an avid pursuer of some of the odder tidbits of Victorian social history. Hayne would think you to be wrong. As Hayne describes it, Lovesey has instead written dismal tomes about an invented past, a writer who possesses a consistency strongly resembling that of Maypo; mildly tasty, but always predictable. A statement by Lovesey that he is writing a fiction that is intended to be a fantasy world that provides the opposite effect of the worlds created by science-fiction writers, a world that "is real and under control," is misinterpreted by Hayne to mean that Lovesey has deliberately set out to produce a universe of lifeless drones, a bad costume-drama without "a spark of life or fantasy." But Hayne cannot be sure if Lovesey's thorough knowledge of Victorian customs ia a joy or a burden; she approves of his knowledge, but it is a knowledge that produces drones. In other words, Lovesey is damned for his strengths; what Hayne perceives as the virtues of Lovesey are identical to what she sees as his vices. Thus Lovesey's singularities cancel each other out, and we are left with nothing.

Hayne's sins, both in her essays on Lovesey and on other writers, are at least original. Most of the bad academics in this volume are carbons of each other, using a sort of Identikit of criticism. The chief components of this Identikit are threefold:

1. *A justification of the work for the "intelligent" reader.* One of the common justifications of the classical ("Golden Age") mystery is that such fictions, although lacking in depth or humanity, made up for their failings as novels by the skill of the author in supplying entertainment for "intelligent" readers, by setting up a puzzle that the reader could solve using his or her wits and brute deductive skill. It is rather odd, then, that the sort of mystery which the critic usually recommends for "intelligent" readers is neither the classical writers or late classicists such as Crispin or Keating, but rather the more cerebral sort of thriller/spy novelist. Thus Ross Thomas is described by Carol Cleveland as a writer whose books "run like well-oiled machines for entertaining readers who have good general intelligence and strong suspicions about the way the world works" (p. 1380). Whether a book is designed to be read by a reader of high or low intelligence is irrelevant to its quality; trash can be as memorable (and, in its undercurrents, important) as "high" literature putrid. That a book is written to be read in the parlour does not mean that it will remain to be read after parlours subdivide into apartments.

2. *The misleading allusion; or, through the past with net and quotation.* Those avid readers of *The Armchair Detective* know that, on occasion, that august journal is filled with bilge about "_____ and the Mystery," the blank being filled in with the name of a Classic Author. We are mercifully free of that sort of entry here, although some entries are certainly questionable. (Ray Bradbury? Samuel Fuller?) What we are not free of is the sort of allusion that makes little sense, when compared to the author under discussion. For, as any writer's characters can be compared to Shakespearean ones, so too can any writer's work be compared to a Greek myth, the number of myths and characters being so vast. One of the interesting games you can play with this book is to score a critic on the number of allusions he/she makes in an essay. Points should be given for the quality of the allusion: low scores for myths (particularly those about poor, bedraggled Oedipus), Christ-figures, and American writers before 1900; high scores for the obscure author used as a reference, or for combining allusions in shotgun marriages. Thus John Snyder would score big for referring to John le Carré's future with

George Smiley as to "explore the Conradian possibilities of this humanly political Janus," and Ian Ousby would also score for his reference to Household as being a successor to William Godwin. If this sort of literary Scrabble proves tiring, you can always shift games and play at determining what a particularly obscurantist critic really meant by a given passage. For openers, I commend the last paragraph of Newton Baird's essay on Joseph Hansen (pp. 727-728).

3. *The critic as God.* Some self-parodies:

> I was fourteen when I read *The Big Sleep*. I have never gotten over it. Growing up, I saw in Marlowe an icon of manhood to which everyone should aspire. The result was sometimes disheartening to my parents, and, in truth, I have had to learn from others. But there was quality in Marlowe, and if I had to do it over again, I would. And so I learned from Raymond Chandler that the form in which he worked was a form in which one could do serious work. All his life Chandler was annoyed at the critics who were inclined to take his work less seriously than he did because he wrote about a detective. I share Auden's belief that Chandler's "books should be read and judged, not as escape literature, but as works of art." Chandler was in earnest. Most of us are. (Robert Parker, pp. 285-286)

> Hough is a crime writer who places the crime story into the philosophical web Dostoevsky wove for it and for which existentialism stretched into "truth." At bottom, though, Hough is a stern critic of the existentialist world-view--but he can make it perform a dazzling death dance across the surface of his narratives. (Larry E. Grimes, p. 821)

There are two ways that critics can play at being God. One is by standing on the shoulders of giants and remarking how magnificent is the view; the other is by standing on the shoulders of the obscure and claiming that one is on a literary Everest. Parker whines; knowing that he is, at best, a minor successor to Chandler, it is all he can do to blubber about the thrills of his adolescence. Grimes, analysing an author so obscure that he has not been published in America since 1969, and that time only for his science fiction (written under the pseudonym "Rex Gordon"), raises this pinnacle of obscurity to Parnassian heights.

Thus we have completed a survey of *Twentieth-Century Crime and Mystery Writers*. Half of this volume is brilliant, and half is quite bad; that this review concentrates on the pedant should not mean that the scholar has no place here. Indeed, the criticism of H.R.F. Keating and George Grella alone make up for a dozen Parkers and Grimes. Those who have written thoughtful essays, who have maintained the right and saluted the deserving, do not need extra praise. It is my purpose here to purge mystery criticism of the pedants, of those who replace depth with obscurity, knowledge with irrelevance, scholarship with scholasticism. Mystery criticism, if it is to rival the best of mainstream criticism, does not need a Larry Landrum or a Joanne Harack Hayne. Let the pedants retreat to the "popular culture" journals, to the subsidized quarterlies, and let those of us who remain ensure that the *second* edition of *Twentieth-Century Crime and Mystery Writers* becomes the fit and lasting monument that the first was meant to be.

BLAME STEPHEN SONDHEIM
By E. F. Bleiler

Frederick Hazleton. *Sweeney Todd, the Demon Barber of Fleet Street.* Introduction by Peter Haining. W. H. Allen, 1980, ₤5.05.

In England the story of Sweeney Todd is something like *Arsenic and Old Lace* with us, a tongue-in-cheek, mock-horror play that is put on whenever the local dramatic group wants a sure thing and does not want to be bothered looking for something better. Sweeney Todd is also something like the Loch Ness Monster, a good story that many people have spent much of their lives in researching which cannot, unfortunately, be proved.

For the past hundred years or so, enthusiasts have been combing the records trying to find evidence that there once was a barber on Fleet Street, London, who murdered customers with a trapdoor chair and then cut up the corpses, which were made into meat pasties in the next-door pie shop. Trial records, early newspapers, city directories, criminal literature have all been searched, but no one has ever found the slightest trace of such a person or crime.

Despite this really conclusive negative evidence, there have been people who believe that Todd flourished (his razor) in late eighteenth or early nineteenth century London. Montague Summers, not a man of very good judgment, thought that Sweeney was a real person, and now Peter Haining has joined Summers, for the conclusion to Haining's introduction states a guarded belief in Todd. Or, at least, that is what the words say. Haining may be kidding us.

As far as anyone knows, the story of Sweeney Todd is of French origin. It first appeared as a description of a "factual" crime said to have taken place in Paris around 1800. An English translation of this text (or so it is identified) appeared in *The Tell-Tale*, a British periodical, in 1823. Haining reprints this English text. Reference is made to Fouché's *Archives of the Police* as the ultimate source, but to my knowledge no one has ever checked Fouché.

Haining, however, also refers to an earlier English version of the story, which his source says appeared in an English periodical, *The Leisure Hour*, for 1795. And here is a typical example of Todd research: the reference seems to be a hoax on the part of Haining's source. I have checked the *British Museum Catalogue*, the *Union List of Serials*, the *Library of Congress Union Catalogue*, and the *British Museum Union List of Periodicals*, and found no trace of such a publication. It probably never existed. The title doesn't even sound like a Georgian title.

Haining goes through the other hearsay evidence for Todd and finds what he considers good evidence for Todd in an American program book for a production of the play in New York in the 1920's. This program book is very specific, with birth and death dates for Todd (1756-1802), and it gives as its source of information an issue of the *Newgate Calendar* for January 29, 1802. It also states that Todd was taken off by John Ketch. This, of course, is such nonsense that I find it hard to believe that Haining takes it seriously. There is no issue of the *Newgate Calendar* for January 29, 1802, and John Ketch died a good 125 years before Sweeney Todd. Since Haining must know Ketch's period, and would have checked the reference, I am inclined to think that he is putting one over on us, and I note that his text at this point is a little disingenuous.

To fill out the book Haining reprints a version of *Sweeney Todd* written by John Hazleton, which version is probably a spin-off from the stage-play. It is a bare narrative of plot and not of much interest. From many points of view it would have been better if Haining had reprinted the real, original text about the Demon Barber. This is *The String of Pearls*, a long anonymous novel printed by Edward Lloyd in 1846-47. Its authorship is unknown. Summers, who gathered rumor and oral tradition among collectors, claimed that it had been started by George Macfarren and finished by T. P. Prest, while Haining roots for Prest as total author. My own feeling, from the samples that I have seen from it, is that this is one more case of Prest's being saddled with an anonymous work, and that Prest had nothing to do with it.

All in all, the present book is not a work that deserves serious consideration. Or purchase.

NOTES ON RECENT READING

The conventional wisdom in publishing is that you lose your shirt if you do volumes of mystery short stories since nobody buys them. Credit two publishers with enough guts and imagination to fly in the face of that way of thinking. Davis has collected five of Erle Stanley Gardner's pulp novelets (1930-41) in *The Amazing Adventures of Lester Leith*, a bargain at $1.75. Leith was one of fiction's great con men, reputed to have "earned" over seven million dollars during his literary life of crime. He donated it all to charity--except for 20 percent which he kept as "expenses." The five tales, all of which were reprinted in EQMM during its Golden Age, are very readable. Best of the group is "Bird in the Hand," Frederic Dannay's choice for the best Leith story.

Another con man is Colonel Cuthbert Clay, who appeared in Grant Allen's *An African Millionaire* (1897), one of the cornerstones in Queen's Quorum. The book contains twelve stories, which originally appeared in London's famous *Strand* magazine in 1896-1897, about Clay's efforts to fleece a South African diamond mine millionaire. Allen was a story teller and, as a result, this work has held up. A bonus are the many illustrations which make one nostalgic for the time when they were such an integral part of many genre books. Thanks go to Dover for publishing this book, which has been out of print for eighty years. The price is $4.50, but this is not bad considering the high quality of Dover's product.

If I seem overly enthusiastic about older material, it is because my experience with more recent stuff has not been too good. Two highly touted Private Eye novels by Brad Solomon, *The Gone Man* (1977) and *The Open Shadow* (1978) were only mediocre. Unreadable was George V. Higgins' *The Digger's Game* (1973). Laughable was Edward Levy's *Came a Spider* (1978), about a policeman's attempt to thwart the takeover of Los Angeles by spiders. Ditto Nick Carter's *The Mind Killers* (1970), about Samuel Sonyoung, founder of Mind Control Techniques, who tries to hypnotize a U.S. Senator to attempt to assassinate the President. He'd have been better off offering the Senator a bribe.

The exception was a good 1980 paperback original from Charter, Barbara D'Amato's *The Hands of Healing Murder*, $2.50. This is a locked-room killing in a room full of witnesses.

Physical clues are well handled. Only unbelievable motivation on the part of the murderer keeps this book from being top class.

NERO WOLFE ON TV: A REVIEW

I suspect that almost all readers of *The MYSTERY FANcier* watched the premiere of the new Nero Wolfe series on Friday, January 16. I wonder if they are as apprehensive as I am regarding the future of this long-awaited venture. The script writers have obviously read enough of the Wolfe canon to include such authentic touches as having Wolfe sleep in yellow pajamas. However, in adapting Rex Stout's 1953 *The Golden Spiders* to the TV screen, they have omitted and changed enough to provide us with a pretty routine hour of entertainment.

In the book, Wolfe uncharacteristically becomes involved in a case at the request of a neighborhood urchin. He becomes serious about it when the young boy is killed. On TV, the boy is merely injured, thereby weakening considerably the emotional impact. Incidentally, in the book the boy gives Wolfe his savings, amounting to $4.30, to seal their bargain. Inflation and TV have brought the amount up to $12.50. Too much of what little time is left to the story, after ads, is given to shots establishing the locale as New York City. For no good reason, except possible shock value, they have dragged in, during the last thirty seconds, the possibility of lesbianism.

The cast is barely adequate. William Conrad is too physical a person to be convincing as the sedentary Wolfe. He appears to be trying to laugh and sound like Sydney Greenstreet, who would have been the perfect Wolfe. He also seems to be trying to puff himself up to seem taller and fatter. Lee Horsley as Archie is only fair, not mature enough for the role. George Voskovec, Robert Coote, and George Wyner are Fritz Brenner, Theodore Horstmann, and Saul Panzer, respectively. Their roles are small, but Voskovec, a fine character actor, contributes a nicely dignified bit in response to some churlish behavior by Wolfe, the gourmet. Alan Miller is Inspector Cramer. Wolfe seems unduly impressed by his ability to get up from an armchair without using his hands. I do not recall this happening in any of the books or novelets.

The most important element missing from this series so far is what makes the books so much fun: the wonderful interplay between Wolfe and Archie. If it is not introduced in future episodes, the series will be in deep trouble.

MISCELLANEOUS MYSTERY MISH-MASH

1. Sherlockians will look askanse, but Nigel Rathbone is the actual name of a young British actor who has appeared in the series *Pennies from Heaven* and the musical *She Loves Me* on PBS television.
2. In the movie *Son of Kong* (1934), sequel to *King Kong*, Carl Denham (Robert Armstrong) is hiding from his creditors. He stays at a boarding house run by one Mrs. Hudson.
3. *Small Genre Department*--Books in which characters discuss or carry out an "exchange" of murders in order to divert suspicion:
    a. Patricia Highsmith, *Strangers on a Train* (1950).
    b. Nicholas Blake, *A Penknife in My Heart* (1958).

c. Fredric Brown, *The Murderers* (1961).
   d. Evelyn Berckman, *Stalemate* (1966).
   4. Since she clearly has always been liberated, I suspect that Helen MacInnes is no friend of the extremists in the women's movement that began about 1970. Was she being prophetic when she wrote in *Neither Five Nor Three* (1951): "She had been worried in case Joe's girl would turn out to be one of those dreary hairy-legged creatures, breathing an atmosphere of boiled milk and women's wrongs."
   5. Remember the Brasher Doubloon, the legendary coin featured in the 1947 movie of the same name, a film version of Raymond Chandler's 1942 Philip Marlowe novel, *The High Window*? Struck in 1787, it is one of the few American gold pieces remaining from the period before the U.S. Mint was established in Philadelphia. The coin was given to Yale University in 1944 and stolen in 1965 by thieves who hid in the Sterling Memorial Library before closing time, overpowered guards, and got away with almost one million dollars worth of rare coins. In 1967 a Private Eye, appropriately enough, traced it through underworld informers to a Chicago area coin collector. The coin was returned, with no questions asked; the thieves were never caught. On January 10, 1981, Yale sold the Brasher Doubloon for $650,000 to an unidentified coin collector in Palm Beach, Florida. The money will be used to help the school build a new library.
   6. *James Bond Department*. In 1963 Aston-Martin Lagonda, Ltd., built a car, the Espionage Special D B-5, for the movie, *Goldfinger*. In 1979, the company introduced the car, minus the 007 features, to the American market. The price was $80,000, though by 1981 it had gone up to $100,000. They have sold about 120 to date, including one to Dean Martin.
   Little noticed was the death on January 16, 1981, of Bernard Lee in London at age 73. He was "M" in the first twelve Bond movies, from *Dr. No* (1962) to *Moonraker* (1979). He played Inspector Valentine in *The Detective* (1954), in which Alec Guinness was Father Brown. He was also Edgar Wallace's Inspector Mann on British TV.
   7. Lachman's Third Law: Avoid books whose titles fit the pattern of *The Quiller Memorandum*, *The Striker Portfolio*, *The Matlock Papers*, *The Bourne Identity*, *The French Connection*, et al. There are a couple of exceptions to this rule: Gerald Sinstadt's *The Fidelio Score* (1965) and Derby Quinn's *The Limbo Connection* (1976), the latter an exciting British mystery in the Woolrich vein in which a movie writer's wife disappears, and he is suspected. Writing in the *New York Times*, Christopher Cerf jokingly predicted some of Robert Ludlum's future titles, the kind I suggest you avoid: *The Holden Penalty; The Norman Cousins; The Heimlich Maneuver; The Columbus Circle; The Hoover Vacuum; The Plymouth Fury* (or, if you prefer, *The Dodge Challenger*); *The Oscar Gamble; the Menachem Beginning; The Dolittle Congress; The Anderson Difference*.

Mystery * File

Short Reviews By Steve Lewis

Edmund Crispin. *The Glimpses of the Moon*. Avon, 1979 (first published 1977), 296 pp., $2.25.

In a recent issue of *Fatal Kiss*, my otherwise splendiferous bi-monthly contribution to DAPA-EM, I thoughtlessly mentioned in passing that I could not think of a mystery I had recently read that was funny to laugh at as well as fun to read. Almost immediately, Charlotte MacLeod's Professor Shandy books were pointed out to me. I've read only the first one, that being *Rest You Merry*, and I shouldn't have forgotten it. The second, *The Luck Runs Out*, is out, and it is near the top of the must-read pile.

But, Ms. MacLeod's efforts in the limited field of comedy detection notwithstanding, I'm forced to say that *The Glimpses of the Moon* is absolutely the funniest detective story I've ever read.

Everyone in it is quite bonkers, you understand, and that's the kind of humor it is. From Gobbo, the drooling local village idiot, on down. The arthritic Major, whose tone-deafness does nothing to inhibit his singing voice when it comes to the lyrical sensitivity of his favorite TV jingles. The innkeeper whose avocation it is to lie abed three-quarters or more of the day. And this is only Chapter One, the tip of the iceberg. Even Gervase Fen is only mildly astonished to find that the head of a pig that he has carried around with him all day suddenly turns out to be the battered head of a corpse.

Or take Chapter Eleven, for example. It begins with Fen and the Major sitting together in an apple tree, the better to view the proceedings below, involving a herd of recalcitrant cows, a motorcycle scramble, several members of the local anti-hunt league, the rector and a thief, and .... I guess you've just got to read it to believe it.

The murders, for yes, some there are, are of a rather bizarre nature, involving not only decapitation, but limb-pruning as well. And there's a "locked room" mystery as well: How did the murderer steal the missing arm out of the tent?

The motivation is probably a unique one. What else could it be in a wacky affair like this but rather unusual, to say the least?

(To be honest, I think Crispin too often lets the story run away with itself. Take P.G. Wodehouse, for example, to see how such nuttiness *can* be kept under control.) (B)

Lucille Kallen. *C.B. Greenfield: The Tanglewood Murders.*
Wyndham Books, 1980, 222 pp., $9.95.

Have you ever noticed how much more you enjoy a mystery novel, say, when the background is a local one, or one you know? Take, for example, Tanglewood. As everyone in most of New England must know, at least, Tanglewood is an annual summer home of the Boston Symphony Orchestra, a small village and environs snugly nestled in the lush green hills of the Massachusetts Berkshires, up near the New York border.

An apparent plot against the orchestra seems to be motivated by more than the usual resentment levied against them by the local townspeople, upset by the yearly influx of gawking tourists. Tackling and solving the murder that eventually results, their second case, are C.B. Greenfield, crusty publisher of a weekly upstate New York newspaper, and his star reporter, Maggie Rome.

It's Maggie who does the legwork, and Greenfield, although long and lean, supplies the Nero Wolfian ratiocination. While their combined detective technique lacks polish and remains determinedly amateurish in style, the two sleuths are most decidedly up to the intellectual challenge of the musical clue left as a dying message--from Ravel's "Rapsodie Espagnole"! That, plus a helpful quote from Shakespeare, and the quiet serenity of one of this part of the country's most charming corners is quickly restored. (B plus)* (*Reviews so marked have appeared earlier in the Hartford *Courant*.)

Stuart Kaminsky. *Never Cross a Vampire.* St. Martin's Press, 1980, 182 pp., $8.95.

As a flight into the past, Stuart Kaminsky's series of adventures starring Hollywood private eye Toby Peters has come now to be a regularly scheduled event. As in his previous four cases, this affair, which introduces both Bela Lugosi and aspiring screenwriter William Faulkner as clients, is fairly dripping with Nostalgia. With a capital N.

The time is January, 1942, just as the U.S. was gearing up for its mammoth forthcoming war effort, and every so often we are obliged to sit down and listen to Peters recite his breakfast menu, brand-name by brand-name, and to read his newspaper along with him, item by item. This litany of places, names, and events, while marginally interesting, becomes very much suspect, however, the moment Peters mentions having listened to a program on the popular radio series "Suspense." As it so happens, the first program in the series, which lasted until 1962, by the way, was not broadcast until June 17, 1942, or not until six months after the events related here.

Kaminsky has put more effort than usual into the plot this time, which includes, very briefly, a locked-room murder, but sloppy and inaccurate time-tabling--not month and year this time, but the time of day--makes it a little difficult to do more than to guess who done it. (C)*

Donald E. Westlake. *Nobody's Perfect*. Fawcett, 1977, 285 pp., $1.95.

I was talking about funny detective fiction a little while back. Standing and looking on from the sidelines, it's obvious that it's much easier to write a funny mystery story when you don't have to work some detective work in to go along with it. Funny crime stories are a lot more common.

Donald Westlake, while he doesn't have a patent on it, does have a particular genius for this sort of thing. The caper story, that is. He's written a number of them, and many of them have starred, if that's the right word, a small-time thief, a crook named Dortmunder. Even his name is funny, but what makes the crimes he and his gang commit so funny is not that they're so badly planned, for they're not, but that all of a sudden, beyond a certain point, everything unavoidably goes wrong.

In this book Dortmunder is hired to steal a painting. He's hired by its owner, who can use the insurance money, but who is naturally reluctant to part with the painting itself. He'd also rather the insurance company didn't get too suspicious.

Somehow, however, the painting ends up in Scotland, of all places, and to save his very hide, Dortmunder has to commission a forgery. And steal that. Which doesn't work out either.

Now, all of this may sound as though it's be very easy to write, but a good part of what makes this story funny is Westlake's way with words, a sardonically understated sort of slapstick, if you will. If Hollywood were to get their hands on it, or from the typewriter of a lesser mortal, you can bet it would end up just being silly.

Westlake also has a well-developed knack for describing a world and its inhabitants where the life of casual, amoral crime is nothing but another plane of existence. It's almost funny, for example, to discover how easy it is to steal a typewriter just whenever you need one, but not quite, considering who always ends up paying for such petty pilferage. Sure. You and me. You better believe it. (B)

Ruth Rendell. *The Lake of Darkness*. Doubleday, 1980, 210 pp., $10.00.

When Ruth Rendell's books involve her series character Inspector Wexford, she writes detective stories, and, as a guess, most of her fans like those best. She also writes crime novels with a psychological bent, none of which carries a character over from one to the next. From all indications, these are the ones the author herself prefers to write. While they are intended less to be read for the sheer pleasure of reading, perhaps, they are not, by any means, any less rewarding for it.

Wexford is not in this one. There are two other major participants in this ironic melodrama as it gradually unfolds. One is a mild-mannered accountant wrestling with latent homosexual urgings, thrust suddenly into an affair with a married woman. The other is a pale, anemic handyman with (he thinks) psychic powers. He is also (we know) a psychopathic killer.

That their paths are doomed to cross, of course we also know. That it makes for such shivery reading has nothing to do with the supernatural. These two unfortunates are so overwhelmed by life, so permanently warped in personality, that they have literally become alien to the rest of humanity, in thought and in behavior, if not in appearance. They are innocents caught up in a monstrous twist of fate. What Rendell renders so convincingly is the fact that even if we were so inclined, there's no way in this world we could ever help them. (A minus)*

Lionel Black. *The Penny Murders*. Avon, 1980 (first published 1979), 160 pp., $1.95.

As if we didn't already know, the age of electronics is upon us. When a wealthy numismatist is found shot to death in an inner sanctorum of his home, completely guarded by the most sophisticated of perimeter circuits and alarms, suicide is the only logical possibility. The dead man had the only keys, and they were found on his body.

Kate Theobald, unstoppable lady journalist, is persuaded by the manservant of the deceased, however, that there is more to the story. Not surprisingly, there is. Some information about the impossibly rare 1933 and 1954 English pennies, which supposedly never left the mint, comes to light, and so do some decidedly noxious warts that had blighted the dead man's personality.

Kate's husband, henry, is a barrister, the son of England's most famous criminal lawyer, and a coin collector of sorts as well. Together, Kate and Henry make a pretty good team, although it is she who does most of the detecting, and he who (so reminiscent of the many pitfalls stumbled into by a certain Mrs. North) stupidly falls into a trap while trying to give her a hand.

The dialogue, as seems common in a goodly amount of British crime fiction, is blunt, terse, and flat. Black has an engaging writing style, and he uses it well to conceal the lack of depth exhibited by his characters. The solution is as up-to-date as today's hardware store, and (surprisingly) it is as easily explained and as obvious *ex post facto* (an exciting phrase from the Latin which means here that, no, I didn't figure it out but either) as most locked-room mysteries usually are. (C plus)

Fred Zackel. *Cinderella After Midnight*. Coward, McCann & Geoghegan, 1980, 334 pp., $11.95.

When private investigator Michael Brennan agrees to help find his client's daughter, he thinks he's working on a run-of-the-mill custody case. Instead, the trail leads him straight into the gritty, grimy pesthole of San Francisco's notorious Tenderloin district.

One of the primary obligations of the California private eye novel has always seemed to involve the public display of some of the sorrier undersides of the once-proud California dream. Here we get an eyeful. We're led from alley to gutter and back again, and just as we've begun to feel there's no escape--and for most of the inhabitants of this noxious world there is not--the trail suddenly takes a surprising twist upward, into the light of day and into the inner offices of some of the state's leading politicians and financial leaders.

Brennan's client turns out to be a hooker, but at one time she was a call girl with powerful government connections. He spots the daughter in a porno film, one she made with a live-in lesbian lover. The mother is murdered, the girl is kidnapped, and the underground revolution is blamed--but we know better. Big Business and Big Government are both involved--the twin Boogie Men that may grab us all yet.

The story is steeped in sour sex and melancholia. There is little to blow away the pervading gloom. The plot is wonderfully convoluted, a mystery addict's delight, but its grip on the reader never wholly takes hold. Why this should be so is not entirely clear. There may be cause for beginning to wonder whether, just maybe, a message like this one may not have been a measure too much for its overpowering means of conveyance to handle. (B)*

William L. DeAndrea. *The Lunatic Fringe*. M. Evans, 1980, 287 pp., $10.95.

The title is a little bit of a puzzle in itself, perhaps. What it's referring to is a group of dedicated election year radicals who have been rallying about the cause of the Democratic presidential candidate.

Not enough information, you say? Take, then, the book's subtitle, which is: "A Novel Wherein Theodore Roosevelt Meets the Pink Angel." Yes, that Theodore Roosevelt--but he's not the one running for President. The year is 1896, and William McKinley is the Republican candidate. Running against him, on the Democratic ticket, is William Jennings Bryan, the silver-tongued orator from Nebraska.

Bryan and his campaign are being backed by William Randolph Hearst, the new publisher of the New York *Journal*. Roosevelt is still only the president of that city's Police Board, and his staunch ally in fighting corruption in the ranks is a young police officer named Muldoon. And it is Muldoon who innocently begins to unravel a plot which, left unchecked, would spell doom for half the city.

These were the days of an entirely different era, politically as well as socially. DeAndrea, whose two previous books have each won him an Edgar award, has caught the flavor well. There is a touch of Horatio Alger in Muldoon, a rough but ready Irish cop, and a warm sense of proud propriety in Katie, his older but still unmarried sister.

Regrettable are DeAndrea's occasional lapses, as in much bad science fiction, into allowing his characters to talk to each other of things it seems they should already know. Worse, as if to emphasize the significance of our vicarious trip back into time, DeAndrea himself finds it useful to remind the reader that these were also the days of the Wright Brothers and of Charles Darwin. Not as characters, mind you--that of course would be too much to dare--but as names dropped only in passing. (Really, now, how often does a name like Carl Sagan, to take an obvious example, get mentioned in any of today's contemporary fiction?)

As a detective story, which is what this is, parts fit, and parts don't. Those that do are often muddled, though seldom beyond repair. Minor inconsistencies in character sometimes have a reason behind them, and sometimes they take the appearance of whims, fashioned to fit passing reflections.

Even so, although the motive for the murder Muldoon and his superior find themselves investigating seems in the end to have been rather nebulous, DeAndrea as the author produces a creditable surprise as to the identity of the killer.

It does not seem enough, unfortunately, to keep his award-winning streak alive at three. (C plus)*

Robert L. Fish. *The Gold of Troy*. Doubleday, 1980, 401 pp., $11.95.

Everyone loves a treasure hunt, and of course the bigger the prize the better. Except that what the prize consists of this time is a large chestful of cheap-looking trinkets, made of what looks like a poor grade of brass.

It's not long, however, before we learn that this is in actuality the famous Schliemann treasure, a priceless collection of golden relics of the Trojan War, discovered by archaeologists over a hundred years ago.

The treasure was lost at the end of World War II in Nazi Germany, but it has suddenly reappeared. Someone has it, no one knows who, and it has been put up for bids in a mammoth world-wide auction. The CIA has always thought the Russians have had it. The KGB has been convinced that it was the Americans who stole it away during the confusion at the end of the war. Each is now sure that the other's security has been breached.

A love affair is also involved, between two people ordinarily worlds apart. She is the newly appointed head of the Metropolitan Museum of Art; he is Russia's leading authority on matters archaeological. Together as they hunt down this small treasure of buttons and beads, their love is consummated, nearly lost, and then wrapped up neatly again in a wild whirlwind of a finish.

The plot machinations come too obviously from the head of the author alone. The characters have little to say in how they're manipulated. As great lasting literature, this would never do. As to why the book is so readable, why it is gulped down so easily and quickly, there is an equally easy explanation. To put it in simplest possible terms, Fish knows how to tell a story. (B plus)*

Richard Lockridge. *The Old Die Young*. Lippincott & Crowell, 1980, 178 pp., $9.95.

In recent weeks a couple of old pros in the world of mystery fiction have shown their fans that they're both alive and well, which is welcome news indeed.

Each has added a creditable entry to the already sizable list of detective novels that have been produced under their names over the past forty years and more. Separately, I hasten to add, and distinctively.

Taking the male member of this pair of famous writers first--a small change of pace, and there's nothing wrong with that, is there?--Richard Lockridge's actual collaborator for

most of his first fifty-five books was, of course, his first
wife, Frances. Together, their most famous creation was the
celebrated husband-and-wife sleuthing team, Mr. and Mrs.
North. When Frances died in 1963 it meant the end of the
Norths as a detective team, alas, but the adventures of some
of their other characters have never ceased to appear. This
is Richard Lockridge's twenty-fifth book as a solo act.

An aptly chosen word, I think. The Lockridge fictional
milieu has always been that of Manhattan and the closer sub-
urban environs, and a closer look would show that very often
forming the basis for the immediate story has been the Broadway theatre.

And so it is here. The mysterious death of a leading man
a little too old for the part he's playing draws Lieutenant
(soon to be Captain) Nathan Shapiro into the world of bright
lights and theatrical temperaments so synonymous with life
along the Great White Way.

Shapiro I pictuee as a sad basset hound who, no matter
what case he finds himself on, invariably thinks of himself
as in over his head. There are no sudden flashes of brilliance
that come in the solving of his cases. He does not believe in
coincidence. A steady flow of evidence accumulates against
the killer.

For all of its brightly crisp dialogue, always a standard
Lockridge trademark, and a brief glimpse or two at modern
morality, this is a mystery still very much old-fashioned in
tone, with little or no action to speak of, but with a good
many speaking parts. (B minus)*

Ngaio Marsh. *Photo Finish.* Little, Brown, 1980, 252 pp.,
$10.95.

And the second half of that description, at least, goes
double for Ngaio Marsh's latest work. Once again on hand to
solve the mystery is her long-time leading character, Chief
Superintendent Roderick Alleyn of Scotland Yard.

Alleyn's first appearance, then as a Detective Inspector,
was--would you believe?--in 1934. This is his and Dame Ngaio's
thirty-first collaboration together.

And, coincidentally, the theatre has played a large part
in many of their cases as well. The connection is not as
strong as it is in the Lockridge book, but there is one here
as well. The scene is a remote hideaway in New Zealand, where
a famous opera singer nicknamed La Sommita has commissioned an
embarrassingly bad opera to be performed, and naturally with
herself in the leading role.

Also involved is a photographer specializing in taking extremely candid shots for the more sensationalistic newspapers.
There is a bare hint of illicit drug-dealing. What the detective work depends most greatly upon, however, is the mystery that surrounds the keys to La Sommita's locked bedroom
after she is murdered.

Alleyn has no Watson along to bounce his theories off this
time--his wife Troy having evidently long ago refused to go
along with the gag--and so some of his deductions are rather
abruptly announced, on what occasionally seems to be mighty
little evidence.

Marsh's writing style lacks some of the sprightly sparkle

to be found in Lockridge's work, but the surprise she gives us at the end is greater. This is only the latest in a long series of plots designed over the years by the reigning Queen of Mystery to catch the unwary reader. She succeeds again.(B)*

Arthur Lyons. *Castles Burning.* Holt, Rinehart & Winston, 1979, 231 pp.

I didn't care much for *The Dead Are Discreet*, the first of several adventures of P.I. Jacob Asch that Arthur Lyons has written up. It was four years ago when I read it, and in these pages I called it "mired in ... muck [with] a plot full of inconsistencies...," and I gave it a "D."
I might have been wrong. (Well, maybe.) At any rate, what *Castles Burning* strongly suggests is that I should not have been automatically skipping all the books he's written since then.
Not that this one started out all that well. Asch decides to give an artist a helping hand in tracking down his son, the spoils of a marriage that went on the rocks some ten years before. The artist's specialty: kinky sex, brought lovingly to life on canvas. Quoting the artist's agent on page three, "We live in an erotic age, dear boy."
But group groping and decor in leather is soon dismissed as a major topic of interest, and thankfully so. The true theme cuts just a little closer to home: alienated children, children with all that money can buy, but junked-out children nonetheless, and maybe therefore. Quoting again, this time from page 190, "They grew up bent because that was the way the light was coming in."
The boy Asch is looking for is dead. The mother has remarried, and now she has a stepson instead. Thanks perhaps to Asch's inquiries, the boy is kidnapped, and Asch's client is blamed.
The characters are vivid and sensitively drawn. Pain and anguish always tend to do that to people, but this time it's real and not simulated. Asch's Jewishness only once comes to the fore, serving briefly to help escalate his growing sense of guilt. In all, the kidnapping serves to create some nicely tension-packed scenes before they fade off into a fairly tame closing.
But only in comparison. For some books the ending would be enough; it'd be what they'd build upon. (A minus)

Aaron Marc Stein. *Death Meets 400 Rabbits.* Doubleday/Crime Club, 1953, 189 pp.

For a pair of quiet, mild-mannered archaeologists, Elsie Mae Hunt and Tim Mulligan seem to run across dead bodies and their murderers with surprising frequency.
Stein has not written up one of their cases in some time now, so they've since retired, with only Stein's chronicles to serve as reminders of what they should be telling their grandchildren.
If, indeed, they ever got married to have grandchildren. They seem to have been inseparable companions, but in this book at least there is not even the breath of a hint of a

romantic liaison between them. Their idea of fun is digging out a thousand year old garbage pit.

Which is what they're doing as this adventure plays itself out against the brightly intense background of sunny/moonlit Acapulco. They are staying at the home of a semi-retired bullfighter who is working now as an honest gigolo--well, as she herself admits, he is giving his American client her money's worth.

But he is killed--and there are plenty of suspects--and she commits suicide. There is what appears to be a "locked room" involved in her death--we readers have suspicious minds, don't we?--and there is, but not one of a sort entirely expected.

Elsie and Tim are hardly professional detectives. They do have, however, a proper sense of curiosity, and digging of course is second nature to them.

But what about the 400 rabbits, you ask? Ah, yes, I'm glad you did. (B)

Kevin Hancer. *The Paperback Price Guide*. Harmony Books/ Overstreet Publications, 1980, 430 pp., $9.95.

A friend of mine gave me some good advice once. "Never," he said, "throw anything away before it starts to smell."

In this age of compulsive collectibles and instant nostalgia, that's not such a bad idea. Besides guides for collectors of antiques in general, there are price guides as well for old baseball cards and old comic books, for example, basic commodities of life that have always given mothers such bad reputations (for throwing them away once our backs were turned). There are price guides for old phonograph records, both 45s and 78s, and yes, heaven help us, for beer cans as well, complete with full-color illustrations.

Joining the illustrious company of these and doubtless many others, the hobby of collecting old paperback books has come now into its own.

Besides the obvious goal of determination and the compilation of current going prices, using some scheme known only to him--there is little or no relation to any asking prices I have seen, but more about that later--the greatest service that Hancer has given the long-time collector is that he has put together in one spot a more-or-less complete listing, by publisher, of all the mass-market paperbound books that were sold originally in drugstores and supermarkets across the country, for prices that from the first were almost always twenty-five cents each. By 1960, however, they had crept upward to the thirty-five cent level, or so. (Now, twenty years later again, check the prices of paperbacks in the bookstores today, if you dare.)

Made superfluous are all the various checklists produced by specialist collectors and appearing in mimeographed forms in various short-lived amateur periodicals over the past few years, signalling the big boom of interest about to come.

Many early paperbacks were mysteries, and mystery fans have collected them in lieu of the more expensive first editions for some time. An added attraction the cheaper paper editions always had to offer was the cover artwork, designed not-so-subtly to catch the would-be buyer's eye, but now categorized as GGA. Good Girl Art, that is, a term coined by a comic book dealer, I think. It speaks volumes for itself, as does the title "Naked on Roller Skates," a book by Maxwell Bodenheim which lists for $30.

Dell "mapbacks" go high, although most of them still lie in the $5 to $20 range, and so does early science fiction. The first Ace Double goes for $100, however, in mint condition, and the book entitled "Marijuana" goes for the same amount. The latter was published in 1951, when you could have picked up a copy, had you but known, for ten cents. Last month I could have bought a copy for a mere $13.

Another friend of mine has a theory about scarcity and price guides, and it goes something like this. Whenever the price of something is forced upward by artificial hype, he says, sooner or later it gets so high that no one wants it. If you have it, your only alternative is to find another fool to take it off your hands. The last person who ends up with it and cannot sell it is thereby crowned the Greatest Fool of Them All.

Check out your basements and attics now.*

The Documents In the Case
(Letters)

From John Nieminski, 2948 Western, Park Forest, IL 60466:
Re TMF 4:6, page 1, line 23--what do you mean,"perhaps"?...

From Charles Shibuk, 2084 Bronx Park East, Bronx, NY 10462:
Dear Jeff,
It's good to hear that TMF will continue to flourish--which is more than I can say for you! (Although the thought of the witty and prescient John Nieminski as editor of TMF does evoke pleasant images.)
I had always thought that TMF was a serious, but not overly scholarly, journal, but the long string of captions attached to the Bouchercon Scrapbook does provide an opportunity to detect an uncharacteristic, though feeble, note of levity on your part. (In other words, I find your attempts at humor laughable.)
Perhaps more of *your* photographs combined with a commentary by John would have been more effective.
I'm sorry to see that your astigmatic condition has deteriorated to the extent that you urgently need the services of an expert ophthalmologist, otherwise why have you confused my first name with that of my friend and collaborator, Mr. Lachman.
Or is your constant reference to me as "Marvin" an example of a massive typo?
By the way, Debbie Reynolds does not particularly care for TMF, and would prefer not to have her name mentioned in your publication.
As far as I'm concerned, I will be obliged to cease writing for your magazine if you are unable to spell my first name correctly.
I can always confine my literary efforts to Bob Briney's *Contact Is Not a Verb*, where I may have been misquoted--but never mis-named!
Yours Truly, Charles Lachman.

From Marvin Lachman, 34 Yorkshire Dr., Suffern, NY 10901:
Jeff:
Practical Horseman, Otto? You look too big to be a jockey.
Congratulations, Al, on getting enough subscriptions to keep *The Mystery Fancier* going. Also, thanks for valuing "It's About Crime" enough to give me a freebie.
Art, Vol. 4 No. 6 was a fine issue. It makes us think

what would happen if *FANcier* folded. I especially liked, even the second time around, John Nieminski's Bouchercon account and the pictures. Perhaps with a drink in my hand, as on page 27, I do look like a benevolent devil. I was glad to see all those additional Jewish detectives that John was able to list. I had written my column while riding my commuter train, with only my failing memory to supply detectives. Therefore, I only came up with the most obvious ones. I've learned my lesson. I should only write where I can consult my notebooks and reference books. (Another Jewish detective, of sorts, is Gaudan Cross in John Dickson Carr's *The Burning Court*.)

Andy, I won't ask why you've moved to Pennsylvania. You're liable to tell me. I'll just wait, since I'm sure you'll tell the readers of TMF in due time.

I'm pleased to see, Newgate, that you're making fewer typos. Was it Townsend the typist or Townsend the professor who corrected the first paragraph to read "things went *precipitous precipitously*"? [*Er....*] That sounds as if I were saying that things went downhill in a downhill manner. What I had written was that "things went *precipitous precipitately*." It was my intent to convey that things *quickly* went downhill. Perhaps a fine distinction, but mine own. Julian, I will appreciate your printing the correction. [*And lay myself open to criticism? Not on your life.*]

Best of luck to you and to TMF where ever you settle and whoever you are.

From Bob Adey, 7 Highcroft Ave., Wordsley, Stourbridge, West
    Midlands, DY8 5LX, England:
Just got TMF 4:5 and am writing at once to pledge my continued support for the magazine. At a time when others such as *Cloak and Dagger* and *The Not So Private Eye* have become irregular and Ethel Lindsay's *Mystery Trader* has ended, we cannot afford to lose one of the big three mainstream magazines (the other two being *Poisoned Pen* and *The Armchair Detective*). Furthermore, by today's post I received news of yet another that hasn't so much died as been stillborn. This is Paul Moy's British project, *Crime and Detective Fiction News*, which Paul now advises will not be published in 1981 because of a number of factors. So, please, Guy, find those 100 subscribers. I'm more than happy to pay the increased airmail sub. of $15.

So confident am I that you will reach your target that I am enclosing a few reviews for your use and will endeavour to be a better correspondent in future (I think I say that every time I write).

Next, some recent comments on recent TMFs.

Barry Van Tilburg's Dossiers are beginning to form a substantial and most useful body of material. Perhaps I can chip in with a couple of points on Dossier #10 (Len Deighton). *Horse Under Water* was in fact the second book in the series, and certainly published over here in 1963 by Cape. (I note that Hubin has the first U.S. publication as 1968.) Also, I have never been satisfied that *An Expensive Place to Die* was in fact about the same central character. There's nothing I could find that positively tied in, and indeed the indications throughout were that it is someone else.

Nothing very exciting on television over here at the moment, with one notable exception. Be on the lookout for a good, long, interesting version of *Dr. Jekyll and Mr. Hyde*. David Hemmings is the hero/villain, and although some of the critics didn't like it, Sue and I did.

One more paperback original to bring to your attention: *Juliet Bravo One* by Mollie Hardwick. This is a spin-off short story volume from a TV series about a woman police inspector with a welfare worker husband. Frankly, I didn't care for the series, but a paperback original book of shorts I'll always have to go for, and there's a second book promised. Incidentally, just to round it off, the rival TV station has also been running a series ("The Gentle Touch") about a woman detective inspector--husband a murdered policeman himself, son a problem, every boyfriend she picks turns out to be bent--you know the sort of thing. Even worse than "Juliet Bravo." Neither of them is in the least realistic.

Finally, to Bouchercon '80. It's the first one that Sue and I have attended, and we really did enjoy it. But so many people to meet in such a short time. I can hardly believe that it's over. So nice to find yourself in a room crammed with people who are not likely to edge for the door when you mention that you collect mystery novels. And very nice meeting you, Guy. (Remember? I was the one who helped lift the crate of Guinness off you. [*Yes, of course I remember. And I must apologize again for bashing you over the head like that; I thought you were trying to* steal *it!*])

The slant of the conference was probably an inevitable choice for Washington, but of course so many of the fans who are interested enough to attend are the ones who are interested in classic crimes, golden age mysteries, etc. Remember the applause when Patricia McGerr suggested that it was time that crime went back into the country house. I doubt whether many espionage novel fans are conventioneers. [*If that last sentence doesn't elicit a long LOC from David Doerrer, I'm a Republican.*]

[*A later letter:*]

Volume 4 Number 6 of TMF has just arrived and been completely devoured. We can all breathe again now that its continued life is ensured, and my $13.50 subscription will be sent to you by Jeff Meyerson.

The stillborn loss of Paul Moy's project is a considerable disappointment, and with *Cloak and Dagger* and *The Not So Private Eye* apparently going through quiescent periods now is certainly the time for John Nieminski to be encouraged (in his madness). I would certainly subscribe, and to what better use could he put his time now that his ghosted Nero Wolfe Saga is completed.

Incidentally, talking of Nero Wolfe, I have skilfully avoided reading of them since an unfortunate introduction many years ago to one of his later efforts (and a poor one at that). But recently I succumbed, read *Fer-de-Lance*, and was immediately converted. A rare combination of excellent detective work, a magnificent character detective, and a genuine wise-cracking sidekick. Just what I need with the space problem I have.

By far the best feature of TMF over the years has been the cliff-hanger serial, "The Strange Case of the Peripatetic Editor," which took another twist in the latest issue (though not entirely unexpected by this stage). For those of us who live further afield (and are thus a little later in receiving our issues), there is the added spice of "will he/won't he receive those precious, painstakingly written reviews and letters before he makes his next move." Even as I write this now, I realise that I am once again dicing with the Scarlet Pimpernel of mystery fandom .... [*No more, Bob my boy; I've finally ended up somewhere that I want to be. I'm going to see if I can't put out at least all of volume 5 from the same address.*]

The centerfold Bouchercon spread was a delight, and you are to be congratulated for the forebearance in your captions. Incidentally, my own position on the floor may well have had something to do with its proximity to the beer cooler (either before or after the event), and it was damned decent of you not to draw the obvious conclusion--at least in print. [*Think nothing of it, Bob. It was the least I could do for a man who had helped me out from underneath a case of Guinness. And, once more, I'm sorry about that bonk on the head ....*] It almost goes without saying that Sue and I enjoyed ourselves enormously, particularly at the get together.

Jon Breen's review of Basil Copper's *The Big Chill* brought out with absolute clarity how difficult it is for Britons to write American and vice versa. I remember with an involuntary shiver an American Holmes story in which the great detective walked "two blocks." You may recall a discussion at Bouchercon over the word "pavement." Over here it means what you walk upon, as opposed to the road, roadway, street, etc., that you drive upon. In many parts of the States, however, pavement means just the opposite--but not in all parts of the States. I think that it was Steve Stilwell who pointed out that in his neck of the woods it meant what it means in England. Strange, isn't it. [*Yes, and stranger still when you realize that you can never believe a word of what Steve Stilwell says, except on those rare occasions when he is saying something nice about me. I may be misunderstanding you, Bob, but we speak of walking so many blocks over here, too. I have never heard the word pavement used in the British sense in this country, and as you yourself pointed out, I've been in a good many parts of it.*]

Last week I watched a made for TV two-hour caper film that sounded as if it would be quite good. Richard Jordan had the lead, and the cast list also included David Niven, Gloria Graham, Elke Summer, Oliver Tobias, Richard Johnson. Entitled *The Biggest Bank Robbery*, you might wonder how it could fail to succeed--but it did, monumentally. The plot was hackneyed and trite, the dialogue unremarkable, and much of the casting (including Niven) was way out. Many loose ends were never tied up and the improbabilities accumulated. Finally, after waiting for a twist in the tail that might have saved the day, there wasn't any. The film just ground to its unlikely end. A terrific waste of acting talent. Give it a miss.

On the other hand, hugely enjoyable was Leo McKern in a long, Christmas-time special entitled *Rumpole's Return* which I urge you to watch. What's more, you can also get author Mortimer's book of the film under the same name, published in a very attractive paperback original from Penguin. I have read recently that McKern is dithering whether to go in for yet another Rumpole series. It seems that his fear is that he may become type cast. Let us hope that it is a fear he overcomes. [*Rumpole's second series began over here last week with an episode entitled "Rumpole and the Man of God." The quality of the series is several orders of magnitude above anything produced in this country.*]

• No doubt some of you noticed in the Bouchercon programme an ad from Greenwood Press for a new bibliography entitled *Crime, Detective, Espionage, Mystery and Thriller Fiction and Film*. Scheduled for November 1980 publication and running to an impressive 400 pages for $29.95. Has any more been heard? Does anyone have a copy?

And what a tantalising snipped of information about Jon Breen's *What About Murder?* Come along, Jon, you really must shrug off your modesty and tell us something about it. I bet it's something I'll want to buy! [*See the following letter.*]

Which brings me logically to the Department of Lost Bibliographical Works. Some years ago Frank McSherry had a book entitled *A Study in Black* complete and scheduled for publication by one of the small but well-known specialist publishing houses (I can't remember which one). I had read some of the text, serialized in the late *Mystery Reader's Newsletter*, and found the subject (fringe mysteries such as occult, science fiction) and Frank's treatment absolutely fascinating, but it never has appeared, and in correspondence with Frank a couple of years ago he confessed that he didn't know what the hold up was, either. [*How about it, Frank?*]

There've been a lot of polls recently, but the one that I'd like to see the results of is which critical works do readers most often refer to. Put it another way, if reference shelves had to be trimmed to the bone, which items would we grimly hang on to. [*Good question; I asked it back in volume one and got maybe three answers.*] Mine would be: Hubin, Queen, *DSS, QQ,* and *In the Queens' Parlour*; Boucher, *Multiplying Villainies*; *Twentieth-Century Crime and Mystery Writers*; Mundell/Rausch, *Detective Short Story Bibliography*; Glover/Greene; Haycraft, *Murder for Pleasure*; *The Mystery Story*; Nevins, *The Mystery Writer's Art*; Haycraft, *The Art of the Mystery Story*; Nevins, *Royal Bloodline*; DeWaal, both volumes--and I doubt if that's all!

From Jon Breen, 10642 La Bahia Ave., Fountain Valley, CA 92708:
 What About Murder? will be out early in April, I think. I still can't give you any info on the price, since Scarecrow hasn't told me. It's a fairly small book, though, and I would guess it would be in the $10-15 range. [*At 200 pages, the Stout bibliography was also a fairly small book, but that hasn't kept Garland from slapping a $30 price tag on it.*] ...

The fine picture spread on the Washington Bouchercon more than makes up for the previous attempt in that line. Though Rita and I have yet to make a Bouchercon outside the L.A. area, we are definitely planning on Milwaukee.

From Bob Napier, 12802 True Lane, #A1, Tacoma, WA 98499:
 Funny you should mention spot illos. I've been thinking that you've been in need of them and I've even worked up a few, but I've never mailed them because I never knew where the hell you'd light from one month to the next. I have this fear of sending anything to an address that you might have vacated just one jump ahead of a batch of tar and feathers. [*Me!?*]

It looks like you don't need me that much anyway. [*Nonsense. Send along whatever you have.*] The graphics in TMF 4:6 were excellent. A perfect cover and very fine section headings. I'm glad to see you pay more serious attention to the graphics in TMF because they go a long way in making the overall package more pleasing to the eye. I have grave reservations (table for two, please, not too close to the crematorium) about your using the same cover every issue. Even a cut-and-paste job would be better than that.

I'd like the names and address of the couple who offered to underwrite the cost of your zine. Anyone who'd give money to an itinerant fanzine publisher sounds like a prime pigeon for my new religion, The Church of Hey, Bob, Do You Need a Couple of Bucks?, Inc.

Nieminski's triple play certainly added an extra flair to your usually fine publication. His Bouchercon article was more enjoyable than many of the events he describes, and his photos helped me to relive the fun of that weekend. How come there were six shots of Ellen Nehr and none of me? And don't give me any lame excuses about taking them all on Saturday night. [*God's Truth, Bob, they were all taken when you were out doing your part for UNICEF, or whatever.*] It seems if the LOL booster gets so much exposure you'd want to balance the scales. Harumph!

Shibuk ... Shibuk .... Didn't the Crew Cuts have a hit of that back in the 1950's.

I'm glad Marv Lachman brought up the subject of Kevin Hancer's *Paperback Price Guide*. I was recently in Portland, Oregon, for a week-end party at the home of Lance Casebeer, editor and publisher of *Collecting Paperbacks?* and owner of one of the best paperback collections this side of Ganymede, who related to us a startling story about the *Price Guide*.

It seems a fellow named Reginald put out a book called *The Cumulative Paperback Index, 1939-1959* a while back and when he made his listings he incorporated a number of ficticious titles and authors to thwart anyone who might try to "borrow" too heavily from the CPI. Apparently Hancer did, and Reginald is now suing Hancer and the *Price Guide*'s publisher, Bob Overstreet, for two million crackers. Lance Casebeer has been appointed as the Court's expert in the case, and to date he's discovered some fifty-four specious entries that Hancer apparently filched from Reginald. Some are really wild: Bantam #472, *The Secret Memoirs of a Chicken* by Andrew B. Stephens; Pennant #66, *Fight for the Plains* by George Ometry (get it? Planes and G. Ometry?); and, Penguin #556, *The Mycenaid* by C. Everett Cooper--supposedly the sister book to *The Necromancer*.

It looks bad for Hancer and the *Price Guide*. Most paperback collectors and dealers have remained dry-eyed about all of this, meanwhile, because the popular concensus is that Hancer's prices are often the result of uneducated and capricious judgements and that the book's main value is as a checklist--false entries and errors notwithstanding. It's a fascinating controversy, nevertheless, and one I'll be following with bated breath.

In answer to Frank Floyd's questions: my favorite mystery/detective writers are Raymond Chandler and Rex Stout and another dozen or so names are tied for third. I've acted in a mystery play, Agatha Christie's "Witness for the Prosecution," in which I played the prosecuting attorney. I found it very tricky because many of my lines were almost identical and whenever anyone goofed his dialogue a critical bit of evidence could be lost, making it imperative that someone try to worm that lost information into the play somewhere else without making it look like a commercial. When the lead actor, who played the defense attorney, dropped three pages of cross-examination one night, it put all of us through the acit test. I prefer comedies--it's easier to make an audience laugh than believe.

From Ev Bleiler, in darkest New Jersey:
On Roylott vs. Rylott. Yes, John Nieminski is right. I was further rebuked the morning after receiving *The Mystery Fancier*, when I found spelled out on my bedroom wall, in blood, with orange pips at decorative intervals, the following high sonnet:
> There once was a doctor named Roylott
> Whose name was too close to Doyle. It
>   Is still pronounced "rile it"
>   No matter how you file it;
> If you change the spelling you spoil it.
>   [*That's a sonnet?*
>   *I wouldn't bet on it.*]

Now, the pronunciation of odd names like Dalziel, Dodgson, Farquhar, Menzies, is something that fascinates me, so I was delighted to see the third line, which I have not come across elsewhere.

From Bill Crider, 4206 Ninth St., Brownwood, TX 76801:
If I can remember to enclose it, you'll be receiving my check for $12. I know I could take advantage of my discount this time, for the last time, but I've decided to contribute the extra $6 to TMF. Charity always makes me feel noble. [*If anyone else out there is overcome with charitable impulses, the new address is 29 South Church St., West Chester, PA 19380.*]
   I judge from your new address that you've found a new venture. Well, you can run, but you can't hide. Charles Shibuk's hit man will find you, even if you're wearing a horse costume.
   Frank Floyd's comments about TV mystery series seem appropriate right now in view of the new Nero Wolfe show. On the very first one, Archie's car blows up. Now how many times did that ever happen in the books? At this point (after three shows) it seems to me that the series is trying to strike a balance between the sort of thing that TV audiences want (or what the producers think the audiences want), like cars going boom and lots of gunfire, and what the readers of the books would enjoy seeing, like the character interplay among the crew living in the brownstone. To me, the third show has done the best job of the latter, and maybe there will be continued improvement. I'm sure you'll get lots of letters about the casting. Briefly, I think Archie is too pretty--you and I know he looks a lot like me [*Saul Panzer looks a lot like you; Archie looks a lot like me, and you know it*] and not some glamour boy; Fritz is too old; Theodore is too old and British; Cramer is ridiculous; and Wolfe, well, the beard isn't as bad as I first thought. William Conrad is getting better with each show, and by the third one he'd won me over.
   Ben Fisher's letter defends "scholarship" pretty well, but I think that what most readers object to is not careful research or deep knowledge of subject matter. What most people think of when "scholarly" articles are mentioned are articles in which the research and knowledge are obscured by a fusty

and pretentious writing style. That's why folks like checklists and bibliographies and tend to skip over articles that begin, "The ontological parameters of the existential commitment of a writer like Dashiell Hammett ...."

The fictitious Bouchercon report compiled by ex-boulevardier Nieminski was well balanced by your own strictly factual account of what actually went on during those days in D.C. You, after all, have the photos to prove your story. Can Nieminski say the same?

The new feature by Jeff Banks was excellent.

And finally, there's a new Nick Carter book on the stands. It's called *The Coyote Connection*, and discriminating readers of all ages are avoiding it like the plague. I'd advise you to do the same. [*I've not yet seen a copy, but someone who has read it tells me that the parts you wrote were outrageously funny. Now, how'd he know who wrote what?*]

From David Doerrer, 4626 Baywood Circle, Pensacola, FL 32504:

You may not believe this, but the copy of TMF 4:5 which you sent to me first class after I called up on the 20th [*of December*] arrived on Saturday the 24th. In the same mail delivery was the copy you sent out, I don't know when, second class! The envelope was slightly torn, but that was all. The address was perfectly legible. Should I send one copy back? [*No, pass it on to some innocent, and maybe we can get him hooked.*] ...

On to TMF 4:5 and 4:6. As you know, I didn't get 4:5 on schedule, thanks to the USPS. I hope that you didn't lose anyone through a similar experience. I obviously couldn't, and didn't, respond in time, but my renewal check is enclosed herewith. Although I'm perfectly willing to take advantage of your generosity in giving credits to letter writers, I wholeheartedly concur in your decision to end this policy with Volume 4. Personally subsidizing the publication of TMF is one thing; doing the same for our various ramblings is something else. If inflation continues, you may well find that you'll have to raise the subscription price again at some time in the future. If so, I might find myself at some time feeling that I couldn't afford to renew, but I would be surprised to ever find myself at the point where I made that decision because I felt that TMF "wasn't worth it." Even after four years' exposure to mystery fandom and fanzines, I'm still surprised that so few readers of mysteries are interested in reading about mysteries.

TMF 4:5--Being neither a Holmes nor a Drood specialist, I can say little save that I enjoyed both of these, and what more can I ask for? The same is true for the articles by Jeff Banks and Carl Larsen. I was never a great film-goer; my one experience with Saturday afternoon programs was a total disaster, of which I remember only the hoard of noisy, unmannered brats in the front rows. Reading gave me far more pleasure with absolutely no pain. I do recall listening to a number of radio serials, including Mr. Keene, but again books won out. Van Tilberg's continuing "dossiers," the reviews, and Marvin Lachman continue to draw to my attention an endless variety of books, of which I can only hope to read a bare fraction.

TMF 4:6--Receiving this before 4:5, I was spared the uncertainty of those waiting to learn if TMF would continue, but my pleasure is no less. Let's hope that this year will at least see you break even. I would indeed like to see another mystery fanzine, particularly one edited by John Nieminski. His report on Bouchercon, not to mention the pictures, is outstanding, giving an unusually lucid picture of this annual event for those who have not yet had the pleasure of attending one. Since I wasn't able to make it to Washington this year, these were the highlights of the issue for me. Jeff Banks' article makes me wish I had discovered *Manhunt* back when. Barry Van Tilburg has hit one of my favorites this time with #34, Philis. I am puzzled that *Dead End* and *Dutch Courage* were not published in the U.S., although Perry's change of American publishers might account for this. Pantheon has published *Bishop's Pawn* and *Grand Slam*, in '79 and '80 respectively. I was also surprised to discover that the "Andy and Arab" books have an espionage background. I somehow never picked this up in the various reviews I've read about this duo.

I trust that the latest letter column has brightened Frank Floyd's day; I know it did mine. [*If that one brightened your day, this one should be good for at least a month.*] I can't offer any suggestions for the recent paucity in this area, save in my own case where it was sheer laziness and a regretable but apparently incurable tendency toward procrastination. In the same vein, I offer the following comments on his suggested topics for discussion as personal opinions only.

I would be hard put to come up with a list of favorite authors which wouldn't be so long that it would appear indiscriminate. I have discovered that my own tastes are quite diverse, often depending on my mood at the time. It would be even harder for me to come up with a list of favorite stories; certainly I could never manage to limit it to five. On this one I'm going to have to pass, at least for now.

On sex and gore, I also doubt if their presence or absence contributes to the *success* of a mystery story, though they may certainly contribute to how wide and what type of audience is reached. Personally, I object to neither unless they are wholly gratuitous or are obviously there only for their titillation/shock effect. As for the TV penchant for blowing things up, I suspect this is wholly for visual effect, aimed at an audience which is not watching for intellectual stimulation. What is more annoying to me (to briefly mount one of my hobby horses) is a TV mystery show where the story requires violence and the producers have "sanitized" its presence to the point of absurdity to avoid the criticism of the PTA vigilantes. The same goes for sex. Move it off camera and, if the story is any good, it won't be missed, but don't "tone it down" to the point where it becomes ridiculous. Two examples: a scene in an "adventure" TV film where one of the good guys is chased across the villain's estate by at least a score of armed men and several guard dogs on leash. Not a shot is fired and the dogs aren't loosed until the pursued disappears over a wall; a scene in a bedroom wherein the female performs with all the virtuosity of a seasoned controtionist in order to emerge from under the bedclothes only after donning her robe or Mother Hubbard, or what have you.

And those querulous mutterings lead into Mr. Floyd's question concerning TV mysteries versus mystery books. There just aren't that many good TV mysteries. The series shows at least need something which will keep the viewers, or at least those in the rating pool, coming back each week, and good mysteries take a lot of work and talent to come across on TV. Unfortunately, too many mystery shows today are attempting to substitute comedy for good story lines, and comedic crime isn't easy.

Can't help with the last two topics at all.

Ben Fisher puts up a good defense of "scholarly" writing, but in citing bibliographies and check lists, plus the importance of thoroughness in research, I think he is missing the point of what I think was being criticized. Unfortunately, though scholarship does not have to be deadly, it often it. There is, I believe, a real difference between thoroughness and accuracy and an attempt to perceive something which isn't there. Some scholars are also, unfortunately, insufferably condescending in their writings about mystery fiction, as when John Halperin writes that "John le Carré is the only writer of espionage 'thrillers' today who is also a writer of literature ..." (*South Atlantic Quarterly*, 79:1, Winter, 1980). A few examples such as this and one might see why mystery fans could be tempted to tar all "scholarly" writing with the same brush. I might add that the letter Mr. Fisher refers to rings no bells. If it was actually deploring the importance of thoroughness and accuracy in research, and criticizing "scholarly" writing for its insistence on these, then Mr. Fisher and I have no difference of opinion. Or almost noen. Could Mr. Fisher have been suggesting that nothing should be published until it's author is assured of total accuracy and completeness? If so, I might quote Cardinal Newman: "Nothing would be done at all if a man waited till he could do it so well that no one could find fault with it."

I wish I could offer Nancy Axelrod some helpful advice, but restoration and repair of damaged books is unfortunately outside my area of specialization. I could suggest that she discuss the problem with knowledgeable librarians in the New Haven area, but I presume that she has already done this. Based on my own experience with books which have been exposed to high humidity, although not actually immersed in water, the smell will fade with time.

Would Elmore Mundell by any chance be the E.H. Mundell, Jr., who co-authored *The Detective Short Story: A Bibliography and Index*? If so, was the checklist he refers to a limited edition of this title? [*Elmore?*] Whether it was or not, surely this was a labor of love. I hope that he has placed at least one copy in an institution where its preservation will be ensured.

Just to close with something out of place. I see that I neglected to congratulate you on getting Walter Albert to take over "The Line Up." I also failed to say that I enjoyed your text which accompanied John Nieminski's Bouchercon photos.

From Al Hubin, 3656 Midland Ave., White Bear Lake, MN 55110:

Although I am overcommitted to reading for the MWA novel committee (more on that anon), I did a fairly thorough browse of 4/6 on arrival, much to my pleasure, noting in the process the various bibliographic tidbits of which I can make use. Particularly good was Nieminski's account of Bouchercon XI; it reawakens my desire to attend the next one, happily nearer these parts (in Milwaukee). Probably there is some Boucherconian (or Townsendian) humor at work which is too profound for these tired cells, but would you explain the persistent references to *Marvin* Shibuk? [*No.*] Anyway, I enjoyed the pictures of Bouchercon too, though they didn't measure up to the annotation in quality. Or perhaps the camera did the best it could with the subjects....

I've served on a number of MWA novel committees, and this year's experience seems odder than usual. For one, almost no "best-selling" mysteries have been submitted (no sign of Buckley, Follett, MacInnes, for example), nor a first novel I thought sure we'd see, if for no other reason than the identity of the author (Margaret Truman's book). And some publishers (Harper & Row, Dodd Mead, Walker, Stein, Dutton, Arbor) have ignored us altogether, whereas Doubleday (out of the dozens they published, both Crime Club and otherwise) managed only two Crime Clubs. I hope to resist a temptation to produce a list of the 1980 mysteries not submitted for consideration; this might answer the numerous fan questions of "how on earth did the committee manage to overlook _____?" In any event, we certainly aren't covering the field comprehensively, and I should complain; I've already got more than enough to read.

The Mystery Library (and my *Bibliography*) seem finally to have gone down the financial drain (carrying with it many thousands of dollars in earned royalties of yours truly's), although every now and again a prospective sign of life is reported to me (most recently on Sunday by John Ball). We shall see. In any event, I expect shortly to be launching an effort to find a publisher for the next edition, which (I hope) will correct/amend the first and update through 1980. In addition, in my madness I am working on two additional features: a settings index (you always wanted to know which mysteries were set in Mississippi, didn't you?), and some sort of guide to which standard reference works mystery authors are included in. In this latter case I am giving fevered consideration to the possibility of including biographical information on those authors not cited in standard reference works, where I can get that information (as from dust jackets or the authors themselves. I expect to be writing many authors directly in search of bibliotidbits. And, if health and sanity continue (return?), I hope to be done with all this late in 1982.

Perhaps the only faintly interesting thing I have to report is this. I share with Steve Lewis (and Carl Larsen and thousands of others, I suppose) an inordinate fondness for old time radio. Recently I acquired two tapes of *Gunsmoke* shows which are most curious indeed. The shows, titled "Texas--Pick up Your Guns" and "Body by the Road"--bear great similarities to the *Gunsmoke* I know and love, but the hero's name is Matt Morgan and he is not played by William Conrad! What on earth have I got? [*Nothing on earth, of course. Those are clearly tapes of programs broadcast in an alternate universe.*]

From Becky Reineke, 1648 Zarthan Ave. S., Minneapolis, MN:

On your insistence that TMF is not riddled with typos, I'll assume the outrageous sum of $14,625 billed to Martin Wooster is another of your leg pullers. [*Nonesense; I assume that Martin's failure to renew to date stems directly from a problem in raising the money.*]

Ben Fisher, Ev Bleiler, and other Droodians will be interested in yet another version of *The Mystery of Edwin Drood,* this one concluded by Leon Garfield. It is already in print in the U.K., and is scheduled for a 1981 (date unknown) publication here in the U.S. by Pantheon. Up to now I've skirted the Dickens issue, though I'm looking on more and more with interest. Whether Mr. Garfield has drawn an effective and believable ending remains to be read, and reviewed, and debated.

The Bouchercon issue of TMF was great! I found John Nieminski's play-by-play quite informative. There was more of an agenda than I expected. And Bouchercon Scrapbook provided the icing. The photo/narration captured the essence of any convention--room parties--while it conjured up visions of family reunions. I'm probably safe in betting every family contains an Uncle Wooster ....

Am I the only one who caught Otto Penzler on the CBS Morning news program last November? I was reminded of it when reading Marv Lachman's delicate treatment of price setting (4:6, p. 32, re: *The Paperback Price Guide*). It looked as if the camera crew was visiting the Mysterious Book Shop, though no locale or free advertising was given. The mysteries Mr. Penzler displayed for the viewers were by your basic authors, Doyle, Hammett, Christie, et al. Prices quoted on said books were steep! It didn't help matters to have the interview conducted by Ray Brady, CBS economist, versus a general interest reporter.

I understand Mr. Penzler wanted to show the Big Names. The majority of viewers would not be impressed with anything less than a first edition *Hound of the Baskervilles* with accompanying high, though no doubt accurate, value. And like Mr. Lachman, I too can't resist comparing prices and rejoicing over a real "find." This pecuniary trait is one of the many inherent in bibliomania. But among my non-mystery acquaintances who watch Morning I spent the rest of the week defending my hobby. No, I am not in it for investment purposes and I can't afford the big bucks. It's a classic case of zealous reading grown uncontrollable. If only CBS had allotted Mr. Penzler enough time to cover the love-of-the-genre aspect of collecting. Surely there are others up and about at 6 a.m. If so, I would be interested in hearing their viewpoints and/or reactions.

From Jim Goodrich, 5 Ulster Rd., New Paltz, NY 12561:

I trust you will cease your peripatetic ways now, so that we can meet occasionally at a nudist resort in the Poconos and discuss hard-boiled dicks. Enclosed is my $9 renewal check; in the past I would have sent $12 with my blessings, but my mad money went to future President Anderson. Am enjoying Carl Larsen's contributions as I'm an Old Time Radio buff. Appreciate your printing that flattering photo of me staring at Martin Wooster on the floor--am thinking: "Youth, why is it wasted on the young?" Frank Floyd: I would say that all the gang (Shibuk, Lachman, etc.) have seen a goodly number of mystery dramas on old Broadway (around the corner on the side streets, that is). Ben Fisher: I doubt that any of us (including this college librarian) have been criticizing scholarship or scholars per se. However, articles extracted from theses or dissertations that flog a topic *are* boring. Randy Cox and Mike Nevins are scholars, but never produce yawn-provoking material for our magazines. Bill Loeser: I like the pieces on films, pulps, radio, and other aspects of pop culture even though I'm a hard-core book reader. Keep 'em coming, Jeff, Steve, and Carl! Trust that Walter Albert has received his copy of *Clues* #1 from BGSU as I have. Jeff Banks: anyone who admires D.O.A., Noah Beery, Jr., and Warren Williams is a person of distinction. Believe Beery entered films at the age of eighteen. Barry Van Tilburg: if we can trust Otto Penzler and his crony Steinbrunner, George Sanders never played Bulldog Drummond. Finally, most pleased to note at the Bouchercon that you had lost a lot of weight and had your squint corrected!

From Jeff Banks, Box 13007 SFA Sta., Nacogdoches, TX 75962:
Here's my check. You knew my answer to the question all the time.

As before, I suggest you raise your price by bigger increments. If TAD is worth $4 a shot, TMF (which I find more addictive) is surely worth $3. [*At least.*]

Also, I think you should drop the contributor copies if money remains a problem. Most of us who write for you are such egomaniacs we'd probably pay you to publish our stuff!

Because I caught the fluff re: Colman-Vance as soon as I saw my piece in print, I read the letters this time. What happened? Most of them seemed interesting! Also I took exception to the Chan "serials" which of course I thought/think I typed as "series." Maybe I should start keeping carbons instead of just rough drafts. [*No need, Jeff. I just types them as I sees them. Of course, with my squint and all ....*]

Dawson and I are working on a chart-article on F. Forsythe. And as soon after the Reagan "tax reforms" as possible, I'll try to find time to do an article on Income Tax Tips for the Mystery Fan. To busy just now working on *Blasted* (the Western your name is going to turn up in [*I've alerted my lawyers*]) to find time even for a real letter.

From Jane Gottschalk, 611 A Franklin, Oshkosh, WI 54901:
The Practical Horseman? So that's how you manage to gallop from one state to another. Those of us who have difficulty just visiting within a state have often wondered. We LOL pedestrians are hard put frequently to make a return Pony Express reply by mail, even when the spirit is willing.

And the spirit, still smiling, wanted to jot as soon as the latest issue of TMF was received, mostly because of the two-fold report on Bouchercon. Thanks to you and John Nieminski. The pictures, with your comment, were a delight, evoking nostalgia for the single Bouchercon I could attend and those I met. Was Bubbles Grochowski front-face camera shy? [*No comment.*] Has Art Scott lost weight? [*Yes.*] Are Bill Crider and John Nieminski as look alikes in person as they appear in pictures? [*They are dead-ringers, actually, and no one ever accused John Nieminski of looking like Archie Goodwin. Foster Brooks, maybe, but not Archie Goodwin.*]

In Nieminski's report of Greg Mcdonald's speech on criticism in the arts, I found Mcdonald's ideas supporting my own observation of much of contemporary writing, including criticism. Romanticism reigns: it claims that unless writing is personal, it is dull; subjectivity dominates objectivity; feelings substitute for standards; an almost illiterate and illogical penned note has more merit than a well-written and well-organized essay; spontanaiety is more precious than careful thought. When will the pendulum swing? Most of the articles, reviews, and letters in TMF do not wallow in the excesses of Romanticism--so do continue.

From Howard Rapp, P.O. Box 432, Gualala, CA 95445:
I have just finished reading Marsh's latest, Photo Finish. Newgate Callendar gave it a rave review. It was a good read but a rather contrived situation. In at least two places Ngaio did not play fair. On page 64, well before the murder, Alleyn is talking to his wife, Troy: "'I think the photographer's here. I'll tell you why.' And he did." No further explanation was made. Again on page 181: "The key and the bag were to be replaced. He explained why." Such things are not in the best tradition.

From Linda Toole, 147 Somershire Dr., Rochester, NY 14617:
Enclosed is my check for volume 5. Is Martin Wooster's copy gold plated? I can't think of any other reason why his subscription should cost so much! [*Ellen Nehr could probably give you a couple.*]
With your most recent move placing you in Pennsylvania, you are almost within striking distance; perhaps I'll be able to meet you someday. I was hoping to meet the elusive (illusive? [*Never*]) Guy Townsend in NYC in December, but all that people there would tell me was that "he couldn't make it." Now, with another move under your belt, a strange idea has come to me--perhaps Guy M. Townsend doesn't exist. This nicely explains the inhumanly frequent moves. Or perhaps GMT is really a group of people, each taking a turn as editor. [*Now, that's an intriguing idea for a hoax, but the last hoax I engaged in nearly left several friendships in shambles, so I'll let it ride. Actually, if you had read John Nieminski's letter from back in 1978 you would know that I do in fact exist; it's Martin Wooster who doesn't.*] I have yet to meet anyone who will admit to having met GMT in the flesh [*Modest, probably*]. I have a letter in the mail to John McAleer and hope he can clear up this mystery for me.
The graphics on 4/6 are exquisite! It sounds (in Mysteriously Speaking) like it was printed in Arkansas, but I hope TMF has the plates.
I enjoyed the Bouchercon material--especially the "Scrapbook." John Nieminski is the best-preserved 89-year-old inhabitant of a nursing home I've ever seen! [*Doesn't look a day over 85, does he?*] Hope his beer coaster is published soon!
I, too, enjoy LOC and will try to answer Frank Floyd's questions. My five favorite authors are: Stout, Doyle, Carr, Chandler, and Poe--for many of the same reasons he gives. Although not mystery/detection, MacAuliffe's Augustus Mandrell has a special place in my heart. Re the sex/gore issue--one strange comment I got (from two different people) on Stout was that "he is much too violent." These people claim to enjoy mystery/detective fiction, but I'll be damned if I know what! Perhaps my expectations of TV mysteries are relatively modest, and therefore I can enjoy them. I found *Ellery Queen* (with Jim Hutton) entertaining, but apparently am one of a very small minority. *Nero Wolfe* (with William Conrad) seems to have promise, but, being a working woman, I have yet to see an episode. Another series I enjoyed was based on *The*

Thin Man, possibly starring Peter Lawford and Phyllis Newman? The only mystery play I ever saw was a revival of Gillette's Sherlockian play, *Sherlock Holmes*. A bit dated, but enjoyable. The only real problem with the production I saw was the actors. Holmes came across as somewhat of a wimp. Kurt Kazenar played Moriarty and stole the show!

I feel that I must address Ben Fisher's letter, since I'm probably one of the people who set him off (my loc 4/5). What I (and I think many other people) object to is *not* scholarship, but rather its presentation. TMF is a source of information, to be sure, but first and foremost I consider it recreational reading. If I want impersonal, formal presentations I can stick to my professional journals. In referring to Bleiler's article in my loc I used the term "impersonal lecture," and so it seemed. Bleiler himself (in the intro) gives us the impression that it was meant for a rather serious journal (*The Dickensian*) and also states he might have written it better today (25 years later); finally, he refers to "more or less scholarly articles" in his opening paragraph. As a case in point for my position, I'm going to use your own article, Mr. Fisher ("Edwin's Mystery and Its History," TMF 4.5). You obviously know your subject well, and I appreciate your knowledge, your scholarship. I also appreciate your tone; it is lighter, more conversational (than Bleiler's). I thought so when I read the article, and I think so now. We *need* scholarship, in TMF and elsewhere, but we also need a (may I say) more intimate tone than one finds in dissertations, journals, etc. The vast majority of the contributors to TMF handle both the scholarship and the tone beautifully. For that I am, and I believe most of the subscribers are, grateful. I hope I've made my view clear. If this is a minority opinion, I will apologize to you and my fellow subscribers. [*Minority opinions need not be apologized for.*] Truce?

P.S. Yes, I *do* "pore over bibliographies." I hope they were written to be used. As for "letters with additions/corrections," I'm sure that (in the interest of scholarship) ommissions/errors should be noted.

From Mike Nevins, 7045 Cornell, University City, MO 63130:
Thanks for the latest TMF, which was full of good things as always. But I was sorry to read about your latest move, which I guess rules out any more of our breakfast get-togethers as I head home from Western film fairs!

I hope your move hasn't kept you from suffering with the *Nero Wolfe* TV series as I have. William Conrad is nowhere near as bad as I anticipated, but Lee Horsley is hopeless as Archie and Allan Miller likewise as Cramer. Worst of all, everything that made Stout's books such impossible-to-put-down treats has been left out of the series, most noticeably the byplay between Archie and Nero, for which the producers have substituted the usual fights and auto chases. And every time the camera goes outdoors it becomes painfully obvious to any viewer who knows the least bit about New York City that the series is being filmed in California. The show is at the rock bottom of the ratings and is bound to be yanked in a few weeks, but I'll keep watching to the bitter end and maintain a week-by-week log as a possible basis for a short article for you. [*By all means, keep the log and write the article. Having long since given up on television, my reaction to each episode has been, well, it could have been worse. But there are so many things wrong with it, starting with the unspeakably bad casting, that no one will watch it with me any more--who wants to listen to a running stream of "No, that's all wrong," "Oh, God," "He'd never do that," "Help me, Lord," and the like. I hope you'll write the article; I'm not strong enough to do it myself.*]

From Myrtis Broset, 204 S. Spalding St., Spring Valley, IL:
I hope you realize you are using up my address book all by yourself.
You are going to write about horses? Should someone warn Dick Francis?
You are going to have to do something about or to Jeff Banks. He has me positively drooling with his latest article, and I'll bet he is not in the least ashamed.
I agree with Frank Floyd that there is often too much sex and violence in mysteries, and the newer the book, the worse it gets. I don't mind this if it follows along with the story, but page after page of it gets boring and makes me think the writer is trying to fill the space.
Where does Frank find the movies on TV that he turns off-- as he says? I haven't found a mystery on TV for months until the opening show of Nero Wolfe. Does anyone think Allen Miller is Inspector Cramer as described in Stout's books?
Never mind about the typos. After reading two interviews with authors, who received millions of dollars for the paperback rights to their books, and both of them stating they cannot spell and depend on their editors to rewrite their stories correctly, I am going to stop worrying about spelling.

From Robert Aucott, 28 W. Waverly Rd., Glenside, PA 19038:
Although you (you?) have ingeniously taken two good friends of mine, and from them created a monster to rival the Chester-Belloc (and although, too, Nieminski's portrait of it/them looks as though he were, really, 89), some of *the Last Cheap Issue* was good enough, despite the itty-bitty print, to drag the enclosed $12.00 from me, for one more year of MF. The MF is not bad; it's even an OK riffle. Except for reviewers who refer to a book as a good (or otherwise) "read." Ugh. What's a practical horse?

From Dick Wenstrup, 1045 Ten Mile Rd., New Richmond, OH 45157:
No. 6 was a feast, particularly the revealing Bouchercon photo-essay. Your Brownie spared no one, reducing even the most handsome face into a Slim Whitman look-alike.
However, your merciless lens posed more questions than it answered. To wit: Is Marvin Lachman black or white? Did surgeons manage to extract that bottle from Martin Wooster's throat? How many verses of "The Face on the Barroom Floor" did John Nieminski (surely he can't be over 75) recite before passing out?
The *big* question remains--what has happened to our *real* editor (the one with the orange beard and glass eye.... Perhaps TMF's next issue will reveal the answer. We'll know something's up if the new, permanent (i.e., for two issues) address is: c/o Locker 13, Greyhound Bus Depot, Hoboken, New Jersey.

From Elmore H. Mundell, 5560 Evergreen Ave., Portage, IN 46368:

I would like to purchase, or see a copy of the piece produced by the University of Texas at Austin as a guide to an exhibit of the newly acquired "Queen" collection of detective short stories (1959, I believe).

Would like to purchase or see a copy of the El Dief (Lew Feldman) catalog of 1954 in which he offers for sale a copy of Poe's 1843 "The Murders in the Rue Morgue."

Can anyone offer an explanation for a 1940 Random House ad (dust jacket blurb) reporting "There Was a Young Man" by Dashiell Hammett?

Would like to get information about copies of Poe's 1843 "Murders ... " sold by Lew Feldman: the one advertised in his catalog; the Joyce copy he purchased in 1973; the Stockhausen copy he purchased sometime after 1970.

From Barry Van Tilburg, 4380-67th Ave. N., Pinellas Park, FL:

These hipocrites who spend hundreds of dollars a year buying and reading books who bitch about spending $12.00 or more for a yearly subscription to a great and very interesting fanzine ought to be shot. The price of this fanzine has been equal or less than most other fanzines out and has better articles and reviews than any others as far as I am concerned. I have gotten more enjoyment for $2.00 an issue than I would from most $2.25 paperbacks. It's too bad some people are just plain cheap. You would not expect it from collectors and enthusiasts of mystery and detective fiction....

About 4/5: I loved Walter Albert's "Line Up"--and I agree with you that *Current Crime* is worth every new pence, but they have screwed up my last subscription (I ordered two years' worth and got about six months worth) so I'm a bit pissed with them.

Also loved Jeff Banks' article on B-movies. During the fifties and sixties I watched Tarzan, Buck Rogers, and Captain Video.

Being a collector, I especially loved the reviews by Steve Lewis and others.

[*A later letter:*]

Sorry for the mistake on the Bulldog Drummond column. You can't win 'em all.

I am glad to see William Conrad returning to television. And as Nero Wolfe yet. The first segment was damn good.

I saw the new Agatha Christie movie, *The Mirror Cracked*. Very good movie with Angela Landsbury playing Miss Marple and Edward Fox as her nephew the Inspector. Liz Taylor was good but Kim Novak was delicious (I was salivating all over my shirt front). I think it was much better than the British "Miss Marple" movies.

From Ed Mahoney, 583 W. 215th St., #C11, New York, NY 10034:

Do you recommend anybody who sells 1960-70 spy paperbacks? [*I dare say this one sentence will net you a booklist or two.*]

From Carl Larsen, 3872 Amboy Rd., Staten Island, NY 10308:

As for 4:5, I enjoyed it thoroughly. Marvin Lachman was as interesting as always, and his closing zebra sentence echoed my favorite lines from Inspector Clouseau. This sort of miscellaneous rambling in which you give an informed and critical mind free rein is one of the things TMF does best. Already the Drood article has drawn response; by the time this is over the whole thing will perhaps be longer than the Nero Wolf Saga. Although Mr. Fisher's ideas are interesting, I must confess that there are several sentences in the section where he treats of the rose motif which I cannot understand. What does it mean to line up a graphic with propensities? Is the ring intended for Rosa because she is virginal, or is she named Rosa because she is virginal? Aside from my denseness, if one is to tackle the symbolic meaning of a crown of thorns, can one ignore the fact that for two thousand years, "crown of thorns" has always (in the West, at least) had the suffering Christ as the crowned one? Again, if Christ *rose* again, why could not another dead man? Symbolism is a thorny field to explore.

There certainly was a bonanza in this issue for nostalgia fans. For those who are not, however, it must have been heavy going. R. Jeff Banks' recall is amazing, as are his statistics on films seen. In my neighborhood, perhaps feeling there was enough modern crime on the streets outside, the theatres ran to westerns, both the singing and the action kind. (How about a few words on Gilbert Roland as the Cisco Kid, Jeff?) Through the miracle of early TV I saw many of the films he mentions and agree with many of his opinions. How lucky in Hollywood was Dashiell Hammett, with both Sam Spade and the Charles family done so well. The issue also had a healthy group of reviews, led by E.F. Bleiler's. Although spies are not my cup of tea, I find Barry Van Tilburg's spy series worth reading. With regard to Bulldog Drummond's film life, I'm not sure about George Sanders, but I'm fairly sure that Ronald Colman, John Howard, and Richard Johnson did play the role. On radio the show had a great opening sequence complete with foghorns and footsteps.

The whole issue makes me hope that your loyal band of enthusiasts will respond in green to your plea for survival....

P.S. Listen, you squinty-eyed little bastard, if you shut down this magazine, I'll personally kick you in the ball [*sic*].

From Bill Loeser, P.O. Box 1702, New Bern, NC 28560:

Although my specialties are invective and diatribe and although Prof. Fisher is a customer of mine, his defense of English professors writing on detective fiction prompts me to take up the cudgels again. First of all, there is no greater fan of scholarship than I. Whenever I read an analytic book in any field, I feel I have been cheated and have possibly wasted my time if the author does not identify and evaluate his sources. At the very least, he has not opened the door for my further reading in his field. My three favorite analytical books in the mystery field are *A Catalogue of Crime* by Barzun and Taylor, *In Search of Dr. Thorndyke* by Norman Donaldson, and *Murder for Pleasure* by Haycraft. Barzun and Taylor were both academics; from the title of Donaldson's other published work--*The Chemistry and Technology of Naphthalene Compounds*--he must at least have had academic training; and Haycraft must also qualify from his long association with H.W. Wilson Co., publisher of various reference books in the field of literary biography. You will note that none, however, are English professors.

From the beginning up to about ten years ago, the study of the mystery was the sole domain of the amateur (one who is fond of [thing]; one who practices a thing [esp. an art or game] only as a pastime, esp. unpaid player etc. [opp. professional]--*The Concise Oxford Dictionary*). [*Oops! Sorry about changing your practises to practices--I'd didn't realize you were using an English source until I had pulled the sheet from the typer.*] They did it for the fun of it, and the professionals--English professors--felt that anyone other than Poe and Dickens--even Doyle--was beneath their dignity. Only when the pop culture boom hit English departments did the professors begin turning their attention to the mystery. And when they did, they produced such things as "The Problem of Moral Vision in Dashiell Hammett's Detective Novels," which *was*, as Prof. Fisher puts it, "deadly" and besides of little if any interest to the reader of detective fiction. I agree with Prof. Fisher that the writing of English professors on detective fiction doesn't have to be deadly, but almost always it is--the only exception I can think of from what I have read is the first chapter of *Adventure, Mystery, and Romance* by John G. Cawelti. The real difficulty, though, is that the professors are concerned with different matters than readers--and not just mystery readers. I suspect that the reader of Shakespeare of Dickens is equally interested in the problem of his favorite's moral vision as is the reader of Hammett. Moreover, the professor is frequently attempting to test, demonstrate, or prove his critical system--new criticism (which is now pretty old, having been in vogue when I was in college; its premise is that an author's life is immaterial to his work); Marxism (Honest! I recently saw advertised a Marxist analysis of the Brontés); structuralism (a professor friend, who professes this, has several times attempted to explain this to me without success); and no doubt others of which I'm unaware. The reader, on the other hand, is an unreconstructed fan of the old criticism. He wants to know about the author's life, what prompted him to write, how he wrote, what his sources and inspirations were, etc. If the English professor will give him this, the reader will be ecstatic, if the professor is doing so with the pleasure of the amateur, for the professor will have the analytical ability and the nose for and access to sources.

As for bibliographies, until the recent ones of Hammett and Chandler, all the good ones--Queen and Rausch and Mundell on short stories; Adey on locked room mysteries; and, of course, Hubin--have been done by amateurs. Hagan was trained as a librarian and not as a mystery reader, and we all know what a mess he made. This, though, I think is attributable to a lack of interest by the professionals.

From Ben Fisher, Box 816, University, MS 38677:
A couple of matters about *Drood*. John Nieminski's letter puts into words one of my own opinions: I always come away from the latest "ending," "solution," "new light" piece with feelings of admiration for somebody else's ingenuity. Ungrateful, John, though, to advocate the Helena-as-Datchery idea-- and at the same time bit the hand that feeds him! (Maybe I misunderstand, and he isn't a high school teacher as his letter seems to imply. [*You do; he isn't.*]) He's right about the Droodians, or Droo-ids as they used to style themselves; there *are* plenty of them. Incidentally, an interesting essay on John Jasper, as a Hero-Villain, no less, is coming out in a journal I edit: *University of Mississippi Studies in English*, new series, I, due, we hope, by late March or April. To look

ahead, the second volume (this is an annual, but the 1980 and
1981 numbers will be out within this calender year) will run
an article on the Dover reprints of Wilkie Collins's novels
and stories. Subscriptions are $5.00 a year, and can come to
me or the Business Manager, English Department, University of
Mississippi, University, MS 38677. Add one more publication
to your library, fans; I expect to publish sometihing in "our
line" each issue. Frank Floyd's enthusiasm for Poe reminds
me, too: the 1982 issue of UMSE will be a Poe issue, and several items under consideration center on Poe's detective tales.

Back to Droodiana. Carl Larsen's letter commenting on Mr.
Grewgious' name reminds me to remind him that Robert F. Fleiss-
ner has recently published some pieces concerning names and
naming in *Drood*. This is a subject that needs lots more work;
in fact, the much broader subject of names in Dickens's work
is open for such readings. After all, in just about all his
major, and in all the minor, fiction, Dickens plays games with
names. How about the name "Helena," in *Drood*? It means
"light," and one of my observations has been that this novel
provides a pretty consistent pattern of imagery (dare I remark
that by such means we might foresee a conclusion, even though
we may not be able to hammer down each detail of that ending?),
if we know that such consistency in literary technique/art appears in Dickens's other novels. Light for Helena is important
because of the wicked Jasper's existing in "shadow," whether
it be in his skulking under trees, in the opium den dinginess,
or in the shadow created by Grewgious' standing between him
and the hearth's--domestic, positive, humane--light when he
imparts news of the broken engagement? Enough on this subject.

Ev Bleiler's letter is interesting, although I'd like to
make a little clearer one point. Just because Grewgious, and
we mustn't forget Edwin himself (othrewise somebody is sure to
remind Mssrs. Bleiler and Fisher what silly jackasses they are),
are present when Bazzard is shown the ring does not mean that
anybody *but* Bazzard--in my opinion--becomes Datchery. Dickens
does make it a point to let us know that the whole showing of
the ring has consequences, both in the text itself and in his
remarks to Forster, his biographer and confidante. Why, then,
show the ring to Bazzard if he will play no future role, related to that little "rose" of a gem? I agree with Bleiler's
ideas about the original cover (it is reproduced in the Penguin of *Drood*) having ambiguities--although, strange to say,
the center depicts roses, with just as many, or more, thorns
as flowers, shaped like a ring, or crown of thorns. Since
Dickens, much more so than, say, George Meredith, among Victorian novelists, was particular about the graphic work in his
books, I'd incline to think this cover is of importance. I
must say, too, I disagree with Bleiler's notion that "Datchery
hates Jasper." The text doesn't say that, although Datchery
is hot on Jasper's trail--for just what we don't know. Or we
don't know how many details there would have been to mount up
charges against Jasper--as the unfinished text does not give
them to us with exactitude. I'm not sure, though, that if
"hate" is the right attitude for Datchery, that it would be
inconsistent in Bazzard. He is interested in dramatics (and
it is ironic that Bleiler uses words like "character" and
"role" in dismissing Bazzard as a candidate for Datchery), and
if signs of "hate" do come across to us as we watch Datchery's

pursuit of Jasper they may result from Bazzard's acting abilities. To say that Bazzard could not be Datchery because that is "certainly no part of his proposed role as agent of Grewgious" is to fall into the procedures of so many previous readers of *Drood*: eliminate possibilities because you don't see them yourself! To conclude here: I have written a much longer piece on *Drood* that might clarify certain matters, at least as they would be consistent with Dickens's earlier methods, were it to see print. One word more: if Bleiler wished that he had emphasized Datchery's "emotional situation" more, I thoroughly concur--but remind him that that situation may be ambiguous because of the element of disguise and role-playing inherent in it.

www.ingramcontent.com/pod-product-compliance
Lightning Source LLC
Chambersburg PA
CBHW031435040426
42444CB00006B/814